CYCLOSPORTIVES
A COMPETITOR'S GUIDE

The authors, ready to ride.

CYCLOSPORTIVES

A COMPETITOR'S GUIDE

Jerry Clark and Bill Joss

THE CROWOOD PRESS

First published in 2011 by
The Crowood Press Ltd
Ramsbury, Marlborough
Wiltshire SN8 2HR

www.crowood.com

British Library Cataloguing-in-Publication Data
A catalogue record for this book is available from the British Library.

ISBN 978 1 84797 244 6

Disclaimer
The authors and the publisher do not accept any responsibility in any manner whatsoever for any error or omission, or any loss, damage, injury, adverse outcome, or liability of any kind incurred as a result of the use of any of the information contained in this book, or reliance upon it. If in doubt about any aspect of cyclosportive, readers are advised to seek professional advice. Since the exercises and other physical activities described in this book may be too strenuous in nature for some readers to engage in safely, it is essential that a doctor is consulted before undertaking such exercises and activities.

Typeset by Jean Cussons Typesetting, Diss, Norfolk
Printed and bound in Singapore by Craft Print International Ltd

CONTENTS

FOREWORD

I do not consider myself a 'true' cyclist. I feel part of the contemporary generation of reborn cyclists – those whose bikes were central to their childhood but had no place in the years devoted to young family and career building, and who, at around forty, found the time and perhaps heeded a subconscious call to rediscover the thrill of cycling.

I have lived for longer in my life without a bike than I have with one; I have never belonged to a cycling club; I have never raced. Yet at fifty-three, my whole life revolves around cycling with a passion that I have at times had to control in the interest of my loved ones!

However, perhaps for these same reasons I do feel myself to be a 'true' cyclosportive rider. I began riding them when you could still enter on the day; when the idea that they might be sold out was unimaginable. This makes me sound ancient, but I am only talking about ten years ago. In that short time, in the UK, cyclosportives have become probably the most popular form of amateur competitive cycling.

This book, devoted specifically to the cyclosportive cyclist in such a specific and focused manner, has been long overdue and I am convinced it will help to make the whole experience both more enjoyable and successful.

They are not as much about results as about personal challenges, accomplished with others. Their selling points are usually the climbs involved, and this is where they really got me hooked. To me, cycling along the flat is two-dimen-

Phil Deeker.

sional, whereas as soon as the gradient rises, the sport acquires its full 3-D character and depth. The climbs in a sportive are feared, yet are central to the whole event. It is where each rider will have to face his or her abilities and limits of determination. The sportive rider may get dropped later on the flat, but if he or she has performed strongly on a climb, stripes will have been earned.

Being of a light build, I soon discovered the 'grimpeur' within. I became fascinated by the games that mind and body played out against each other when climbing, even on the relatively short UK climbs. The longer the climbs lasted though, the deeper I plunged into the mystical magic of gaining elevation with pedal power. It was always a painful process, but as fitness and strength increased, I became more sensitive to the subtle beauty of smoothly pedalling upwards.

The real drama and beauty of climbing, however, became apparent once I started riding the cols of the French Alps. The Étape du Tour, which is to cyclosportive riders what the Tour de France is to professionals, became the highlight of my Sportive calendar for several years running. Riding up a 20km, 8 per cent climb with several thousand others on closed roads is a unique experience: each rider is alone, battling with physical and emotional demons, and yet is intimately bonded with everyone else around. No one is 'winning', and no one is being 'dropped', since there are thousands more down the road. Yet at the end of the day, each rider will have achieved something quite special, in his or her own eyes, and in those of many others. That rider might have completed their first ever Étape; they might have got a first gold medal, or been placed in the top five hundred. Every one of those is an equally immense achievement.

Therein perhaps lies the key to the mass appeal of the cyclosportive.

Since my Étape rides I have gone on to ride up hundreds of mountains, and I can revisualize almost all of them. Each col climb has been a meeting, not a battle to be won or lost. Depending on fitness, mood and weather, meetings with the same col naturally vary. I have held several 'meetings' with the Mont Ventoux, and the story has been very different each time. What never changes though, is that they always require the cyclist to give everything as he or she confronts the mountain, and themselves. Each ascent presents a further examination, and this is often a very humbling experience. The cols that are the 'stars' of a Gran Fondo, L'Étape or the Dragon Ride will be there waiting for us each year, and will always offer us a new, unique opportunity to test ourselves and perhaps discover something new about ourselves.

Perceived limits within ourselves partially define our own personal reality. There are so many things in life that we imagine to be impossible. Everyone sets their own limits, and these limits can be the source of much fear. Free ourselves from fear and we can transform our lives for the better. Physical fitness can go a long way to acquiring self-confidence that will push back the threatening barriers of fear. In our generally sedate, safe existence we have few moments that allow us to test ourselves individually whilst being within a group. The cyclosportive event provides a perfect opportunity for this. I highly recommend it to everyone who has been infected, even just lightly, by the beautiful bug called cycling!

Phil Deeker, 2011

DEDICATIONS

Jerry Clark:
There are many people to thank for supporting not only the writing of this book, but for enabling me to ride and enjoy the people, places and experiences that come from sportives.

In no particular order: my wife Ali for her patience and support in all those miles spent training and the time competing in events. My daughters, Olivia and Sienna, for constantly reminding me that nothing is as important as them. To my grandmother, mum, dad and Nigel for everything, and to Peter and Brenda for their support.

To Bill Joss (BJ) for luring me to the bike in the first place, and for his coaching, encouragement and company throughout our friendship.

Pete, Phil, Yngve, Matt, Jason, Rob and Mark for sharing all those rides – may there be many more.

Mickleover, Derbyshire, 2011

Bill (BJ) Joss:
I have ridden many miles, in many countries, with many people over many years, and to attempt to acknowledge them all would be to risk offending someone by omission. So I will simply extend my thanks to the unnamed companions (they know who they are) who braved dark frosty mornings or rejoiced in sunlit sultry evenings as our pedals turned through every experience cycling has to offer.

I will, however, pick out one name, and express my special thanks to Jerry, with whom I have shared an extraordinary journey in business, racing cars, an infatuation with 'the beautiful machine' and now co-authorship of this book.

My appreciation must also go to Debbie, who has always taken the view that 'if I can do it, I should do it'; and crucially over the past decade to Mr Stephen Young, without whose orthopaedic expertise I would never have been able to ride many of those miles at all.

Thank you one and all.

Whatcote, Warwickshire, 2011

ACKNOWLEDGEMENTS

The authors would like to thank the following for their valuable contribution to this book:
Phil Deeker for his insightful foreword (www.centcolschallenge.com).
Dave Cranny for his time and digital photography skills.
Wayne Murray for his expertise and various contributions on stretching and the avoidance of injury (www.mickleoverchirohealthclinic.com).
Peter Hall and John Clark for proof reading, and John Fegan for his contribution on training camps.
Rob Smith and Ali Clark for modelling.
Rapha Publishing for kind permission to use an extract from 'Le Metier' by Michael Barry and Camille J. McMillan.
Ben Mason and Andy Blow at VOTWO Events for their contribution on an Organiser's Perspective (www.votwo.co.uk).
Ian Stuart for kindly liaising with the organizers of the Maratona Dles Dolomites event.

Each cyclist fights an internal battle. Some fight on the bike because it gives them
purpose and simplifies the complexities in life.
Others escape. Others ride to fill a void.
Others battle childhood disturbances. Others pedal for fitness or weight loss.
We each have our reasons.

From Michael Barry and Camille J. McMillan *Le Metier* (Rouleur, 2010)

The authors of the following text are not professional medics, trainers, physio-
therapists, coaches, sports psychologists or physiologists. In fact we aren't quali-
fied at all, other than by dint of mileage covered, personal participation, effort,
research, dedication, successes and achievements, along with some disappoint-
ments, accidents and failures along the way.

We are just a couple of bike riders like you, the reader, who felt we could contribute the accumulated information, experience, knowledge and 'been there,
done it' stuff of two decades or more to help the growing group of sportive
enthusiasts who now make up the vast majority of the active cycling fraternity,
and whose numbers are multiplying at an astonishing rate.

But a quick health warning: check with your GP before taking up a rigorous
training regime, and give it a while before you attempt to emulate the astonishing
accomplishments of your professional bike rider heroes without plenty of training
and years of dedicated training, not to mention outstanding natural talent and
ability.

Take our advice and recommendations as they are intended: simply the
thoughts and observations of enthusiastic and reasonably capable colleagues.

Enjoy.

INTRODUCTION

Dawn breaks on a clear, chilly morning somewhere in one of Europe's undulating and spectacular landscapes: the UK's Yorkshire Dales, the Italian Dolomites or perhaps the ultimate cycling location, the French Pyrenees or Alps.

A thousand, sometimes many thousands of competitors assemble in the start pens, chatting nervously, making final, imaginary bike adjustments, setting and resetting computers, fiddling with helmet straps and race numbers. The anticipation, excitement and nervous tension is palpable in the cool, crisp air.

Every rider feels the same: the élite group looking to set a new record, the charity riders focused on delivering for their chosen cause, the leisure cyclists for whom this, their first cyclosportive, is the pinnacle of their own personal fitness journey so far.

Every one of them harbours personal doubts and fears; the nerves jangle until the event starts – and then the adrenaline kicks in, the legs begin to turn, and the fitness, the preparation and the well practised routines take over.

The riders are all part of the same growing wave of enthusiasm for the amateur's only real taste of what the professionals live and breathe every working day; for just a few hours each and every one of them will experience the highs and lows of the world of the bike racer – the camaraderie, the competition, the crowds, the lung-searing ascents and the thrill of the fleeting, euphoric descents at breakneck speeds into the depths of the valley.

Each competitor will feel what we have felt ahead of possibly the hardest sportive of them all, Styrkeproven in Norway: 540 kilometres of everything cycling and the forces of

Excitement builds at the start of the Maratona Dles Dolomites, Italy.

A stunning descent.

Anticipation ahead of the challenge: Étape Caledonia, 2010.

nature can throw at a human being. We both remember the final moments before the start, the sheer magnitude of what we were about to attempt looming in front of us, the doubts, the anxieties, the imaginary injuries all vying for attention in those tense final seconds as the clock ticks down to the start time….

Twenty hours later we stand at the finish, completely drained but elated at having completed the toughest sporting challenge we have ever faced.

The cyclosportive, from here onwards called the 'sportive', is the fastest growing mass participation cycling event in today's cycling calendar. With thousands of sportives globally there are now hundreds of thousands of bike riders regularly competing in a range of events of all lengths and profiles. Single events vary from 100

participants to almost 40,000 aiming for gold, silver or bronze age-group standards covering distances from 100km to 550km.

Accessible to all, the sportive offers the dedicated amateur the opportunity to train for and ride in a timed, mass participation event with almost all the ingredients of a pro bike race. Fully supported with electronic timing, feed stations and medical back-up, a sportive brings together cyclists of all abilities in a friendly but focused environment, and successful completion brings a strong sense of achievement.

This book is intended to offer essential advice to riders at the start of their sportive career, and also provide valuable coaching to more experienced riders who want to maximize their potential.

CHAPTER 1

THE CYCLOSPORTIVE – ORIGINS AND EVOLUTION

Innocuously and incongruously located on a wall in what is now a TGI Friday's restaurant on Boulevard Montmartre in Paris there is a small plaque commemorating a conversation that created the most famous event in cycling, and arguably in the world of sport:

> A few months later in 1903, fifty or so intrepid individuals set off at 3:15am on a dark Paris night to ride the first Tour de France …

Of course the Tour is by no definition a cyclosportive; it is perhaps the most famous, most punishing race in all theatres of sport, but it is almost certainly true that the Étape du Tour, the spiritual descendant of that very first Tour de France stage, is to many minds the most prestigious sportive. It is certainly the most over-subscribed of all sportives, and most riders have this event in their sights as an event to ride at least once.

Many of the essential elements of the sportive are present – professional organization, a carefully selected route to challenge and bring out a range of capabilities, a package of logistic support along with the challenge of the clock, and the ever-present threat of the broom wagon (the dreaded truck which sweeps up the slower, struggling and injured riders who fall to the back of the field). Most of all there is the anticipation that comes from knowing that the greatest

cyclists in the world will be covering the same kilometres just a few days later, albeit at a rather faster pace.

Cyclosportive – a Definition

The term 'cyclosportive' is derived from the French *randonnée cyclosportive*, and signifies a long-distance, mass participation, timed event in which riders race not against each other but challenge themselves against distance, terrain and the clock. So a sportive is part randonnée and also part road race: riders have numbers, and times are usually published by the organizers. The biggest and most prestigious events attract thousands of competitors; the biggest of them all, the Cape Argus Pick 'n' Pay, sees up to 40,000 riders jostling for road space and battling fierce headwinds round a stunningly beautiful coastal route in South Africa.

There are now many thousands of sportives taking place around the world, offering a fantastic opportunity to experience cycling in every conceivable environment.

Arguably the first, and still to many one of the toughest, sportive is La Marmotte, first held in 1982. Taking in five of the most fearsome ascents of the Alps, it may not be the wisest choice for a first event as it will test the most dedicated and accomplished of riders. Like L'Étape du Tour, La

This is real mass participation: the Trans Alp Challenge.

Marmotte sees up to 25 per cent of its eager starters retire or swept up as the true extent of the challenge hits them, and the realization dawns that those missed winter extra training miles were, just as we say in this book, necessary after all.

Whichever is the toughest, most scenic, longest or famous, and whatever the origins, the sportive is now the fastest growing mass participation cycling activity in the amateur rider's calendar.

The Essential Ingredients

Distances, locations and course profiles vary, but all events will offer common ingredients: support and logistics, distance, location and profile.

Support and Logistics

A sportive should be well organized and easy to enter, and the basic essentials for rider safety, welfare and enjoyment will be covered, including:

- Changing facilities and toilets at the start and finish
- Pre-published guide times for gold, silver and bronze standards by age group category
- Timing chips to allow logging of progress and overall times
- A route card with comprehensive directions in case signs on the route have gone missing
- Multiple feed stations offering water, energy drinks and food (bananas, cakes, bread rolls, fruit)
- A pre-start briefing and some pointers on weather and road conditions, route changes, rider etiquette and other potential hazards specific to the course
- A minimum of basic mechanical assistance and rider support facilities at the event start and around the route
- An emergency telephone number
- First aid stations around the course
- A broom wagon(s) – a support vehicle(s) able to get you and your bike to the finish in the event of any accident or mechanical problem, or fatigue
- Post-event results.

Distance

Typically a long course will be around 160km (100 miles), with a 'short' route of 110km (70 miles) offered either as an alternative goal or as an escape route in the event of problems on the longer ride. It is worth bearing in mind when selecting a first event, or even when training towards a more ambitious sportive, that an event with multiple route options could be a sensible choice.

A perfect climb: good friends, traffic free.

The short route in a sportive is likely to miss out the toughest climbs, yet still deliver a varied and challenging outing, which is partly why the sportive has become so popular so quickly, as everyone can participate and find their level.

Location

A well-planned sportive will try to utilize safe, traffic-free roads wherever possible, and will incorporate scenic routes and well known landmarks such as major climbs, or 'cols' in European countries.

The route may use narrow roads, and the road surfaces may be rougher and more variable than usual. Consider these factors when choosing an event and when preparing your bike – tyre choice, inflation pressure, spares to be carried all need to be thought through carefully. It is possible, for example, that a sportive course such as the Exmoor Beast which takes place in late autumn will be accompanied by some pretty wild weather, and road surfaces will be strewn with gravel or thorns. At the other end of the scale, an event such as Quebrantahuesos in northern Spain includes many kilometres on beautifully smooth tarmac with long climbs and terrific descents.

Profile

All sportives are designed to present a challenge. Part of that challenge must be the act of hauling varying quantities of human body mass, machine and cycling gear up gradients against the force of gravity, otherwise known as 'climbing'! Climbing is to some the absolute essence of cycling, yet to others the most feared and dreaded element of the sport. Look carefully at the route profile and the pattern of the climbs when selecting an event, and match the severity to your ability and ambition.

A 'typical' sportive of 160km is likely to feature several notable climbs of up to 10km or more, and will offer between 1,500 and 3,000 vertical metres of climbing across the course of the event. 1,500 to 3,000m in 160km doesn't sound much, but then factor in gradients of between 5 and 25 per cent and you will probably find yourself grinding up a total of over 50km in a granny gear (the smallest cogs at the back of the bike) with a few minor lumps and bumps thrown in to unsettle your rhythm, and just for good measure 30°C to 40°C of summer sun. Be aware that any event showing over 2,500m of climbing is a warning sign for a tough sportive, and needs to be treated with respect: a training plan geared towards peaking for that event should be allowed for.

So choose the right event with the right profile for your objectives, and think and plan for the specific conditions and roads. To illustrate the variation between events we have shown two 'typical' sportive course profiles below: the first is acknowledged as one of the toughest and best organized events on the European calendar, the Maratona Dles Dolomites held in Italy each July (www.maratona.it/en); and the second is the Shakespeare 100 sportive held in September in the UK, a challenging, scenic and enjoyable 100-mile (160km) sportive running from Stratford-on-Avon down into the Cotswolds and back (www.shakespeare100.org.uk). Both are challenging events, but the course profile demands a different level of preparation and strategy; more on that later.

The overall aim of our advice and therefore of this book is to help the reader finish an event without needing an oxygen tent and a stretcher, having given everything possible on the day without causing permanent physiological damage. With the right preparation any physically fit individual should be able to tackle a sportive with a little left 'in the tank' and with enough strength to celebrate their achievement at the finish line.

Preparation and Planning

Plan your event nutrition and ride strategies carefully to map on to the specifics of the event itself, and think through what and how much you need to carry on the bike. The

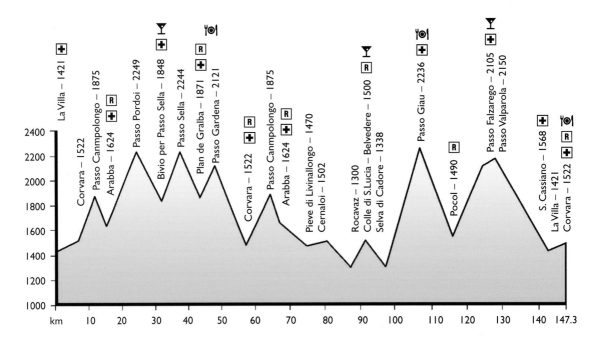

Profile of the Maratona Dles Dolomites in Italy in July.

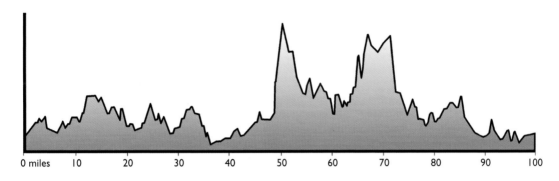

Profile of the Shakespeare 100 Sportive in the UK in September; total climbing 1,720m.

rest – timing chips, massage points, mobile mechanics – may or may not be present, so again, plan your event strategy accordingly. You should ensure that you can deal with at least minor mechanicals yourself, and should carry enough basic nutrition to complete the event should a problem arise. Interestingly Mark Cavendish, the Tour de France sprinter, said recently that even he, with comprehensive and constant race support available, always carries his own supplies in his back pocket, and that this has allowed him to win a race on more than one occasion when feed bags ('*musettes*') haven't materialized.

Take responsibility for your own food, clothing and bike to ensure that if any of the core ingredients are missing you are still able to complete the ride.

An Organizer's Perspective

Organizing a successful sportive event involving hundreds or even thousands of participants is a complicated business, and comes down to managing the sometimes conflicting demands of riders, sponsors, venue owners and local authorities. We asked VOTWO (www.votwo.co.uk), organizers of the Silverstone Sportive in the UK, for their insight into what it takes to arrange a successful sportive:

Choosing a location
When selecting a suitable venue we have to look for one which can cope with the number of riders anticipated in terms of access, parking, toilet facilities, registration and amenity areas, and which also offers a safe collecting and start environment, preferably off the road. This is a challenging task, especially with an event attracting over a thousand competitors.

The course
Once the venue has been identified and arrangements finalized, the organizer then has to plan a course which finds a balance between challenge, enjoyment and safety, whilst

considering the number of turning and hazard points that will require marshalling and signage. As most event organizers rely on volunteer or part-time staff for marshalling roles, they then need to be provided with detailed instructions on where to position themselves and when. This is a very time-consuming but critical part of the task, when a 100-mile

Tour of Britain 2009, 26th fastest finisher.

route may well have seventy-five road junctions to navigate through.

When the route is set, the relevant local authorities are then made aware of the event so that they understand what is happening in their area, and are able to raise concerns or objections and provide information on road repairs or other likely issues.

Promoting the event

We then turn to the marketing and promotion of the event, trying to reach as many potential entrants as possible, providing comprehensive information and allowing early and straightforward entry. This activity requires constant liaison with sponsors and event supporters looking to promote their own interests and brand on the back of the event itself. As an organizer, this is where the gambling begins in terms of the level of investment in advertising and promotion, which has to be recouped through increased entry levels and participation.

In the background there is organized chaos as staff are booked and scheduled, medical cover, insurance, equipment (such as barriers, portable toilets and timing chips) are arranged, and everything is carefully scaled to the rate at which entries appear to be coming in. On that note, it is incredibly helpful if we can gain visibility of entries at an early stage, so that we can plan the logistics to suit. This will in turn improve the quality of the event and the experience for the riders, and minimize any issues which arise on the day.

On the day

When the day of the event arrives, the work really begins; we generally start at about 03:30 in order to get the course signage in place. We don't do this the day before as experience has taught us that the locals and other helpful souls have a habit of removing or altering signs on their way home from the pub, or just for a laugh …

The competitors start to arrive, and the process of registration and starting gets underway. The key element for us at this stage is to make sure the riders find their way quickly and easily to the car parking areas, registration tables and toilets as required. It is unbelievably helpful if competitors actually follow the directions and instructions, as this keeps everything running smoothly.

It also helps if everyone brings their documentation, as this keeps the registration process running to plan.

All underway

Once the bulk of the riders are out on the course, we experience a strange feeling of calm as the stressful preparation work begins to reap rewards. If all goes according to plan, we then begin to see riders arriving back with smiles on their faces. Once everyone is in, it is a matter of collating and publishing results and photos and handling any queries or feedback that comes in. Once again, from our perspective it is important that riders let us know when changes occur – for instance if they opt for a different distance, or even drop out completely.

After a tidy-up (including as much as possible on the course itself) and the recovery of all the signage, we head off with our heads full of changes and improvements for next year. Feedback from participants is very helpful – but we mean feedback, not just negative criticism! Putting on a sportive can be extremely rewarding when the feedback is good, and you can see how much everyone has enjoyed the event, and what people have achieved.

Experience Says …

- Think through your specific aims and objectives before deciding on a sportive to enter. Do not set yourself a challenge that is too far beyond your current capability
- Study the course profile, distances and route details before the event in order to set your pace strategy. If you go off too fast in an event with major climbs in the last half of the route you are asking for trouble
- Plan your event strategy in advance – what to carry, how to ride, who to ride with
- Carry route directions/map so that you can be self-sufficient if a problem occurs
- Pay attention to the briefing so that you are aware of hazards, changes and road conditions
- Make all your arrangements well in advance – don't leave things until the last minute
- Be able to deal with minor problems yourself, so carry basic tools, puncture kits and essential nutrition.

CHAPTER 2

THE BIKE AND EQUIPMENT

A Brief History of the Bike

The bike is often said to be the most efficient man/machine combination ever invented, delivering the highest and most energy-efficient return of all machines powered and employed by the human race. In simplistic terms the basic design of the bicycle has been around for a long time; historians will argue as to the precise moment in engineering evolution when the bike was born, and who was responsible for the invention, but one thing is for sure: there are few who still believe the famous drawing in 1493 by a pupil of Leonardo da Vinci is anything other than a fake.

The fundamental principles of bicycle design had probably been agreed by the mid to late 1800s, but an endless stream of improvements and enhancements continued for a century or more to give us what we, the twenty-first century sportive rider, would regard as our ideal machine.

Incredibly, in the early 1900s the US Patent Agency kept every US patent in just two buildings, and one of them was completely dedicated to bicycle patents.

For the purposes of this brief history we have chosen to start with the Van Drais German 'Running Machine' patent of 1818, while acknowledging the major contribution and developments of inventors such as Kirkpatrick Macmillan of Scotland, the Michaux family of France, and countless others who took the design forwards and evolved the modern machine.

The first truly commercial bicycle venture was founded by the Starley family of Coventry, England, who built and sold the 'Penny Farthing', or as it was correctly known, the 'Ordinary'. They followed this with the 1885 'Rover', perhaps the first machine which could be said to be the modern bicycle.

Kirkpatrick Macmillan's bicycle brought together several of the critical elements that remain in place today: two small, equally sized wheels with the rider in the middle

ABOVE: Da Vinci or amusing hoax?

RIGHT: Elegance in motion!

Familiar lines – a hundred years ago!

Emancipation on two wheels.

Colnago C40 – the benchmark?

MILESTONES IN BICYCLE EVOLUTION		
Year	Invention	Country of origin
1818	Von Drais 'Running Machine'	Germany
1840	Macmillan rear wheel drive	Scotland
1845	Thompson – pneumatic tyre	England
1864	Michaux 'Boneshaker'	France
1869	Harrison – calliper brake	England
1870	Starley 'Ariel' Ordinary	England
1870	Grant-spoked wheel	England
1877	Starley – differential gear	England
1879	Lawson – chain drive	England
1885	Starley's 'Rover' – the first complete modern bike	England
1886	Mannesman – steel tubing	Germany
1888	Dunlop – manufactures pneumatic tyre	Scotland
1896	Hodgkinson – early derailleur	England
1949	Hercules – indexed gearshift	England
1951	Campagnolo – modern derailleur	Italy
1978	Specialized – foldable clincher tyre	USA
1983	Avocet – first bike computer	USA
1984	Look – clipless pedals for road	France
1985	Shimano – indexed 'SIS' gear shifting	Japan
1990	Shimano – integrated brake/gear levers	Japan
2009	Shimano – electronic gear shifting	Japan

A vision of the future.

between them, with a rear-wheel-drive system and a steerable front wheel which is independent of the transmission. The Starley family added a geared drive train and the chain itself.

Since those nineteenth-century beginnings there have been periods when design and technology have moved rapidly forwards, and sometimes things have remained static for decades. Materials have evolved and components have become more sophisticated and inexorably lighter, but it is still amazing to note the similarities between an early bicycle and a modern-day racing machine. In no other field of technology is the relationship so clear.

As is evident from the table above, since 1990 there have arguably been a few advances in materials and refinements, but relatively few ground-breaking inventions and innovations.

Into the Future

The Holy Grail of future componentry might arguably be a breakthrough in drive-train design, in which crank arms, chains and cogs could be replaced by a smooth, variable transmission belt system, which senses the rider's pedal cadence, effort and speed, and automatically changes gear. Tyres will become lighter and more puncture resistant, frames will become lighter, and wheels will also shed weight, becoming more rigid and streamlined to cut through the air more aerodynamically.

Happily for us, as authors of this book, the sportive rider is still likely to have to supply the muscle, aerobic engine and willpower required to complete a successful sportive, and most competitors' budgets will keep them away from space-age prototypes for a while to come!

The Sportive Bike: Characteristics and Selection

Having already said that man and machine are the most efficient means of mechanical propulsion on the planet, it is unfortunate that many would-be riders, bike shops and well meaning 'experts' seem to conspire together to bring this sublime partnership between human sinew and metal right back down to earth.

It may not be possible to measure precisely by how much the wrong bike, the wrong fit and the wrong equipment detracts from the rider's performance, but if slower speed, greater energy consumption, fatigue, pain, discomfort and reduced enjoyment are factored in, we could estimate at least a 30 per cent efficiency loss. For example, it is said that clipless pedals as opposed to traditional pedals and toe straps improve pedalling efficiency by up to 20 per cent. Put another way, if you get the equipment, the fit and the overall formula badly wrong, you will be throwing away up to an hour or more across a typical long course sportive route, and will expose yourself to an increased likelihood of injury.

The good news is that this book is going to show you how the opposite can also be true, in that if you put everything together into an integrated, correctly specified package, your performance will be enhanced, and the pleasure and satisfaction you gain from your riding will be massively greater. Jean Bobet, brother of Louison Bobet, the three-times Tour de France winner, in his book *Tomorrow We Ride*, describes the sensation of cycling when everything is working in harmony as 'la volupté'.

ABOVE: *The clipless pedal, a 1990s development giving improved pedalling efficiency.*

LEFT: *A traditional toe-clip pedal.*

So in an effort to help our readers reach 'la volupté', we will take a look at the various components and essential elements that make up the perfect combination of bike, rider and equipment.

What a Sportive Bike Must Be

The sportive bike needs, in a sense, to be 'all things to all men': it needs to deliver a lively but comfortable ride,

A top-end, modern sportive bike.

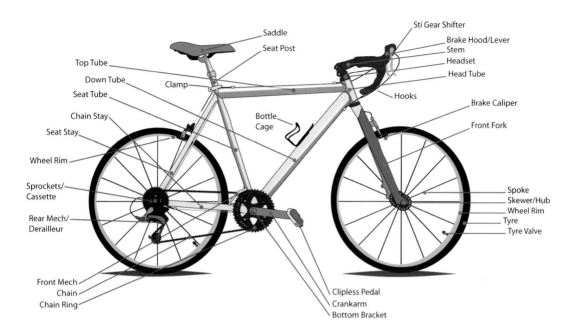

Principal components of the bike.

climbing capably but able to drive forwards at speed on the flat. It will look like a race bike, but it needs more 'relaxed' geometry to offer the comfort necessary for an amateur to cover a long distance over multiple hours on varied road surfaces.

As such, a sportive bike will probably have a longer head tube and slightly upturned stem to position the rider higher at the front, thereby reducing strain on the neck, shoulders and back. The top tube may be shorter than a race bike, and the wheelbase may be longer for greater stability.

The equipment and fittings on the bike may focus on comfort rather than all-out performance: thus the handlebars may have a shorter drop (the height difference between the saddle and the handlebars), the tyres will be at least 23mm wide, and maybe even 25mm to give a softer ride and more puncture protection, while the saddle should be comfortable and designed to minimize pressure on the 'sensitive' areas.

Wheels should have a combination of strength, rigidity and flex, and will usually have between twenty-four and thirty-two spokes. (We discuss the merits of different types of wheels later in this chapter.)

Nowadays many sportive bikes will feature a 'compact' chain set with two chain rings at the front (probably fifty-tooth and thirty-four-tooth) and ten sprockets or cogs at the back, ranging in size from around twelve up to twenty-five, twenty-seven, or even twenty-nine. The argument rages between the more traditional set-up of a 53/39 front chain-ring combination matched with a typical 12/25 rear cassette, as opposed to a 'modern' compact set-up

featuring a 50/34 and 12/27; each rider will make his or her own decision, but we are both firm believers in compact gearing for long, hilly sportives. Some riders still prefer a triple chain ring set-up because it offers a very wide range of gears, albeit at a slight weight penalty. A typical triple chain ring configuration will feature a 53/42/34 combination, which in conjunction with a 12/25 or 13/26 at the back will cope with almost any terrain.

It interesting to note is that on the famous Mortirolo climb of the 2010 Giro D'Italia most of the professional *peloton* were using compact gearing with a 50/34 double chain ring, and some even had a twenty-seven- or twenty-nine-tooth sprocket at the back. Even the pros need some mechanical advantage to help them on their way!

A sportive frame is likely to feature the following angles, give or take a little:

- Top tube joint with seat tube = 73/73.5 degrees
- Top tube joint with head tube = 73/73.5 degrees.

These are probably the angles which give the optimum compromise between speed and comfort in a bike frame.

Women-Specific Frames

The anatomy of a female rider is, as may be evident to most people, different to a male rider. Most notably, a female rider may need a shorter top tube in relation to the seat tube as her reach may be shorter in proportion to her overall body length. Most manufacturers now produce 'WSD' ('WomSpecific Design') versions of their sportive bikes, and

ABOVE: *Compact 50/34 chain rings.*

RIGHT: *A Campagnolo 13/29 rear ten-speed cassette.*

we would recommend that a female rider bases her selection on one of these to start with.

Fortunately for the novice or non-technical amongst us, all the main manufacturers have recognized the need to produce pre-specified sportive bikes, and we would recommend that you select one of these for a first sportive bike.

To explain the wisdom of that recommendation and to show the bewildering array of choices to be made, we will start with the material a bike can be made of.

Frame Material

The main materials for a bike frame are steel, aluminium, carbon and titanium. However, at risk of opening up a national debate and alienating advocates of one material over another, we want to say that we don't think the material a first sportive bike is made of should be the critical deciding factor. What is far more important is that it has the right geometry, fits properly, and is equipped for the job of riding long distance, multi-hour events with substantial amounts of

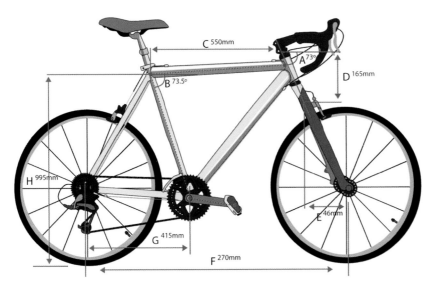

The geometry of a typical sportive bike.

climbing involved. So for example, a slightly heavier steel-framed bike with relaxed geometry and compact gearing will probably perform better for the average rider than an ultra-light carbon-fibre model with race geometry and a traditional 53/39 tooth, 12/25 sprocket set-up.

It's all about the individual rider, of course, but our advice would be to concentrate on the overall characteristics and equipment, rather than the material.

The main materials and their characteristics are as follows:

Steel

Steel has been the traditional choice for most of the 150 years or so of bicycle evolution, being relatively inexpensive, easy to manufacture and work, reasonably light, flexible, resilient and comfortable. Steel frames are widely available, although have become less fashionable in the last couple of decades other than for urban 'fixies' (bikes with a single fixed gear) and among traditionalists and collectors.

A steel-framed bike will be durable and will be available in a very wide range of geometries and specifications. When choosing a steel-framed bike, select at least Reynolds, Columbus or Dedaccai tubing (these names will appear on the frame somewhere) and you will be able to buy a steel-framed bike that weighs not a lot more than carbon fibre or titanium. A good quality steel frame utilizing the steel mentioned above will last for many years (subject to protection from rust); however, lower quality steel tubing will be heavy and prone to corrosion. On the plus side, steel frames are more easily repairable than other frame materials.

Aluminium

Often considered to be the best choice for entry level or first bikes, aluminium is lighter than steel; an aluminium frame may deliver a harsher ride, but it will accelerate fast and respond sharply. It is often coupled with carbon-fibre forks and sometimes carbon seat stays (the frame sections completing the 'triangle of the frame' that houses the rear wheel) to soften the ride. Aluminium may have a 'shelf life' of only ten years or so as the alloy can corrode, fracture and break down with constant wear and stress. It is reasonably priced, light and rustproof, however it doesn't absorb shock as well as steel, titanium or carbon fibre.

Titanium

In some eyes titanium is perhaps the ultimate frame material – a legacy from the world of supersonic aircraft and the space age, it absorbs shock and gives a comfortable ride as well as being light and stiff. Non corrosive, it is impervious to damage by water, is highly workable, and has many of the positive characteristics of steel, but is lighter and with greater stiffness. Titanium is now seen as a niche material because it is used by specialist frame builders and is expensive; however, as a long-term investment it may make a great deal of sense.

Carbon Fibre

There is little doubt that if you ask most sportive riders, they would say that their goal is to own and ride a 'top-end' carbon-framed bike. Ultra-light, nowadays straightforward to mould (or weave, to be more accurate), a carbon frame delivers a responsive and comfortable ride with most of the desired characteristics in a sportive machine. Again, however, its down side is that carbon fibre can deteriorate under repeated stress, and lower priced, lower quality frames may be less durable. Having said that, most manufacturers have now achieved significant progress in the manufacture or 'weave' of carbon fibre, so this is less of an issue than say, ten years ago.

Carbon fibre is the stuff of jet fighters, Formula 1 cars and the Space Age; it is stiffer laterally than it is vertically, so the frame doesn't flex when you pedal strongly, but it delivers a good degree of cushioning while still being responsive. And of course to most eyes, it looks great. One word of caution: carbon frames are not easy to repair and are prone to snap in the event of a major impact.

Our Recommendation

Materials selection is a matter of individual choice, but if we were to make a recommendation we would probably advise starting out on a relatively low-cost aluminium-framed bike, and upgrading to a carbon frame when you are sure that sportives are something that will continue to motivate you. The first machine can then be used as a training or winter bike. We would probably aim at a budget of between £500 and £1,000 for the first bike, moving up to anything from £1,500 to £3,000 for a second, higher specification event bike.

We are often asked for guidance and advice on buying a second bike in particular, and the most common mistake we encounter is when a rider upgrades to a new machine that offers very little enhancement over the first. There has to be a 'step change' in the quality of the overall components, otherwise it may be better just to upgrade a specific items such as the wheels, group set or handlebars.

The Hierarchy of Spend

So how much should you spend, and what should you spend it on? For a newcomer, and even for experienced cyclists who haven't focused on the technicalities of cycling, the choice of bike can be bewildering, and with online buying becoming more prevalent, expert advice isn't always available.

Remember, the bicycle is the second critical component in the equation after the rider, and making the wrong choice can have serious physical, performance and financial consequences. So get it right first time: seek advice and follow the guidelines in this book.

Most manufacturers have a range of sportive-specific bikes available with a wide range of specifications, but for

A fully specified, complete sportive bike.

most riders budget will be the first criterion to consider. At the 'bottom end' it should be possible to buy a basic sportive bike for around £600; at the top it's perfectly possible to spend £6,000. For the purposes of this book we'll focus on the 'average' rider, for whom the purchase of a sportive bike is a major expenditure and who has a budget of £850. For this budget we would recommend buying a fully specified, complete bike from a recognized brand – you can find them from their advertisements in cycling magazines. For the latest bike tests we would direct you straight to the pages or online areas of the magazine Cycling Weekly (www.cyclingweekly.co.uk). Most major, and many specialist manufacturers and brands are covered in their extensive programme of road tests.

There will be compromises in a pre-specified package, but the chances are that you will benefit from the buying power of the major brand and will get a specification which is designed for the job and works together well.

So that said, how should you spend your hard-earned cash? While carbon is probably the material of desire, remember that the golden rule is to get as good a frame as possible as the first priority; other components are quick and easy to upgrade or replace, but the frame will have more longevity. So for example at a budget level of £850 you will probably be able to choose between a very good aluminium frame and a low-end carbon one.

Ride before you buy if at all possible; most bike shops will let you do this, even some of the online retailers, and you need to get the feel of different materials, geometries and set-ups.

In short, spend your money according to the following priorities:

- Frame
- Wheels
- Group set (gears, chain rings, brakes)
- Finishing kit (handlebars, seat post, stem).

If you are putting the specification together yourself, first buy the best frame you can afford relative to the overall budget, next choose a good set of wheels, and then compromise on the rest if you have to. A chainset or a set of gears can be upgraded easily and individually at a later stage when cash becomes available, and you know more about what you need and want.

Assuming you are happy with your choice of frame, if you want to upgrade then our first recommendation is to start with the wheelset, as you will get a greater performance return from an upgrade on these than you will with anything else. Without getting technical, not all wheels are

---

THE ENDLESS PURSUIT OF LIGHTNESS

Although we know, as we write, that our advice will be ignored, don't let weight be the main deciding factor in the choice of an all-round sportive bike; save that until you have completed a few events and are ready to take on L'Étape du Tour or La Marmotte, and the training and lifestyle regime that goes with that decision.

Every rider we have ever met (including the two of us, we will admit) spends too much time worrying about shaving a few grams off the weight of the bike. The reality is that these miniscule savings are simply lost in the overall equation for the vast majority of amateur riders – who would be far better served by adjusting their nutritional intake in order to shed a kilo or two of body fat. The outcome would be dramatically more beneficial to event results and an awful lot cheaper as well....

---

the same: the speed with which a wheel comes up to its maximum revolving speed will be different, the aerodynamics will vary, and the 'flex' (the side-to-side movement when the wheel is under load) will be different for every set of wheels. You also need the optimum combination of characteristics for the style of riding that you do, your weight, and the power output you generate. Hubs are a key part of the decision as well, and rider weight will influence this decision perhaps more than any other factor as it is a fact that heavier riders wear out hubs and bearings faster than a lighter rider. Finally, modern wheels may well feature 'bladed' spokes to improve aerodynamics.

Second-Hand Bikes

With the popularity of online auction sites to add a new dimension to buying and selling used items, along with the tried and tested 'Small Ads' sections in *Cycling Weekly* and other magazines, the newcomer to sportives can find a wide choice of used machines in varying states and conditions.

There is no doubt that fantastic value for money can be had by buying a higher specification bike for the same budget as a pre-packaged model, and remember, bikes are the same as cars: ride one out of the shop and it depreciates by at least 25 per cent immediately. But buying second hand comes with its own challenges: if you are buying privately, then make sure you take down the person's home address and telephone number; and if you are picking up the bike, then arrange to meet at the person's home address. Genuine sellers won't mind you carrying out these checks – remember that if a deal is too good to be true, it normally is, so walk away.

If you do buy second hand, make sure the specification is clear, and ask as many questions as you need to make sure the bike is suitable. Items that are often forgotten are:

- True length of top and seat tubes (these are difficult to measure)
- Length of cranks
- Length of stem
- Sizes/range of rear sprockets.

Also, try to establish how much use the bike has had, as bottom brackets, wheel hubs and other components may be worn. Our experience is that buying a bike from a genuine cycling enthusiast is usually fairly safe, so ask what type of riding the seller does, and how many other bikes he or she has.

Whichever way you decide to buy a bike, to get the best out of it you will need to consider various factors, and in particular its component parts.

Assessing a Bike's Component Parts

Wheels

Sportive wheels need to blend strength – which often means a greater number of spokes – with lightness and responsiveness. So an ideal sportive wheel may have between twenty spokes at the front and thirty-two at the back, either bladed (aerodynamic) or traditional (round).

They will preferably be 'clinchers', with inner tubes and outer tyres, rather than the confusingly named 'tubulars' in which the tyre is glued to the rim and has no inner tube. Clinchers can be repaired quickly and easily (with practice, it takes less than five minutes) while tubular tyres can't be repaired or replaced instantly unless you have pre-glued tyres as spares, or a support car happens to be at your beck and call. Our resounding recommendation for sportives (especially for those of you new to events) is to ride clinchers – even though there is perhaps a performance benefit

High performance, mid-range wheels.

ABOVE: Lightweight clincher wheels.

BELOW: Deep-section carbon clincher wheels with an aluminium braking surface.

We have personally suffered the tragedy of having a pair of hugely expensive, top-end carbon racing wheels literally destroyed during the 550km Styrkeprøven event in Norway as a result of the effects of water and road grit creating an abrasive effect between brake blocks and rims.

Again, if the budget will stretch to it, for flatter sportives you may wish to consider using deep-section wheels – but beware as they can be unnerving in side winds and difficult to handle. But they do look great …

As we said earlier, it may not seem apparent at first, but the time a wheel takes to come up to speed varies enormously, and the characteristics of flex and aerodynamics create a huge performance variation between wheels: just watch a group of riders on a downhill stretch freewheeling to see the difference a good pair of wheels and hubs makes.

Tyres

There is a huge variety of tyres on offer from hundreds of manufacturers. Leading brands all make a range of tyres suitable for sportives, so we recommend keeping to one of these as a safe bet.

from tubulars, and arguably they puncture less frequently. Nowadays with modern clinchers, the rolling resistance is less than it used to be and the puncture protection is greater; if you have a puncture the ability to repair and ride on is, in our minds, the critical factor.

Make sure you buy the best wheels you can afford; many regular sportive riders have two sets, one for training and one for event day. The gearing on both should ideally be the same: it makes sense to train and race with the same ratios. If you can afford a second set of wheels, then these should be lighter, stiffer and more aerodynamic than the training wheels, but above all, they should be suitable for the rigours of sportive riding over long distances. In particular, our experience would point to using wheels with an aluminium braking surface (as opposed to carbon) as the braking performance and longevity of the wheels are superior.

A sensible choice for sportives: fast rolling and puncture-resistant.

The tread pattern of an ideal sportive tyre.

A sportive tyre needs to be puncture resilient but without an excessive weight penalty, and it needs to have as low a rolling resistance as possible. The subject of tyre pressure prompts endless debate; we recommend using a pressure of between 100psi and 120psi, depending on rider weight and conditions on the day. A heavier rider, say of 85kg or over, will almost certainly benefit from an increased tyre pressure. Once rolling, the tyres will heat up and the air inside will expand; so be careful to consider what the tyre pressure will end up at. Just for interest, when we were riding the 2007 Étape du Tour, Greg Lemond mentioned that he felt 100psi was absolutely adequate as a balance between grip, rolling resistance, comfort and puncture resistance.

Select tyres on the basis of several factors: width, tpi (tread per inch), durability, puncture resistance and recommended pressure. Nowadays many tyres are reinforced to reduce the risk of punctures, and we would recommend a 23mm-width, Kevlar-reinforced tyre for most events, with a tread pattern rather than a 'slick' profile.

Inner tubes should be durable rather than the lightest available, and we also recommend carrying a few glued puncture repair patches, as well as two inner tubes.

Groupset

The group set comprises the main mechanics of the bicycle, including the chain rings, sprockets, cranks, brakes and derailleurs. The group set is typically a matched and integrated set, and it is wise to stay within a pre-specified set of components because incompatibilities are everywhere and there is nothing more frustrating (or dangerous for that matter) than climbing a major sportive climb with gears jumping or sticking.

Weight is a consideration here, but more important to the sportive rider is the choice and range of gearing; although we both ride 'traditional' 53/39 gearing during some training rides, for sportive riding we recommend a compact set-up, with two front chain rings of fifty and thirty-four teeth, and ten or eleven rear sprockets or cogs ranging from twelve teeth to twenty-nine. One manufacturer has just released an even more useful addition to its range, offering a 13/32 rear cassette, which should get even the weariest sportive rider up any ascent. Some sportive riders still prefer a 'triple' chain-ring set-up, and there is nothing wrong with that selection. Our experience simply says that we can achieve an adequate range for even the toughest climbs with a 50/34 groupset, so why carry the extra weight, increase the opportunity for mechanical faults, and maintain additional hardware?

To climb a serious sportive ascent comfortably, most riders will utilize a thirty-four chain ring at the front in combination with a twenty-five tooth sprocket or cog at the rear, and modern technique advises a higher cadence (pedal revolutions) or 'spinning' technique, rather than pushing a bigger gear ('mashing') when climbing.

A highly versatile sportive groupset.

If a triple chainring is fitted, this will give an even greater range of smaller gears (albeit with a weight penalty and with slightly more mechanicals to go wrong or go out of 'synch'). Some triples can give similar gear ratios to mountain bikes, so getting up any mountain should be possible.

For most sportive riders, a traditional group set featuring fifty-three or a fifty-four chain ring at the front, and 11/25 at the back, may well leave you struggling unnecessarily on the climbs – too often the authors have seen competitors walking in the last third of an event as a direct consequence of trying to push too high a gear early on in the sportive.

Finally, while a couple of millimetres may not sound a lot, the length of the cranks should be correct for your leg length; short cranks might be 165mm, long ones 175mm, but this small differential makes a lot of difference when translated down through the pedal stroke. The modern trend is towards longer crank arms, but this may slow down pedalling cadence in some riders.

Finishing Kit

The sportive rider will suffer in terms of comfort and possible injury if stem, seat post and bars are not set up correctly.

Handlebars should be, broadly speaking, the same width (measured from outside edge to outside edge) as the shoulder width of the rider; this allows the chest to expand properly and provides the optimal riding position for the arms and hands. Sportive bikes may well have a shallower 'drop' on the handlebars to enable the rider to adopt a lower position on the bike but without straining their back.

The stem should be the right length to achieve the optimal reach position on the bike, and will probably rise slightly to give a more upright stance.

Most sportive bikes will be set up to give a more upright seating position than a thoroughbred race bike might; this will be partly a matter of personal choice (not to mention flexibility), but will usually result in the rider having a back angle of around 45 degrees to the top tube rather than the professional racer's near-horizontal riding position.

The drop from the top of the saddle to the top of the handlebar stem is again about personal choice and flexibility, but typically might be a couple of centimetres on a sportive bike; so the seat post needs to have enough adjustment to cope with this. It has now become fairly clear in wind-tunnel tests that in fact the width of the rider's profile is at least as, or more significant than the rider's height over the bike, so try to narrow your profile rather than emulate the pros with a flat back over the top tube. That is why Time Trial bikes and bars tend to pull the rider's shoulders inwards, thus narrowing the profile. Naturally, if you can ride comfortably while both low and narrow, you will have a significant aerodynamic advantage.

A typical set-up for bars, stem and brake hoods.

Saddle to handlebar drop is a very personal choice.

Saddles

The last word on components must go to the most delicate area of the cyclist's anatomy: the choice of saddle. Once again this is of personal, particular choice, and no two anatomies are the same. But it is essential to minimize pressure on the delicate parts of the rider during a five-, six-, or seven-hour, or even longer, ride.

In general terms, 'less is more' when we are talking about saddles for male riders; contrary to popular myth, a narrower saddle with a smaller surface area is usually better for most men, the point being that there is less surface contact with the rider's anatomy and therefore less chafing, rubbing and friction. The same is not the same for a female rider, however, where women-specific design saddles tend to have a greater surface area to spread the weight and take pressure off specific areas of the female anatomy. Female riders should definitely select a WSD if they are contemplating long hours of training and competing in sportive events.

Modern saddles often have cutaway sections where the base of the perineum rests in order to dissipate pressure, and most female riders will adopt a women's specific saddle since it is designed to deal with the specific physiology of the female form.

At this point, let us issue a strong health warning: saddle choice, fit and comfort is vital to comfortable and successful

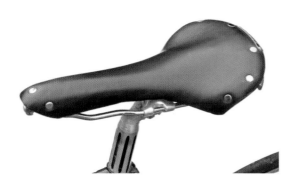

The choice is yours, but make sure you are comfortable.

sportive riding. While further research has now begun to dispel fears about potential impotence in male riders as a result of hours in the saddle, there is no doubt that the wrong shape and style of saddle can, and does, cause a range of problems, from minor blisters and chafing through to more serious issues needing medical attention. So do not compromise on this component, and invest in some good saddle cream for the inside of your cycling shorts to aid comfort and, importantly, prevent sores and chafing, which can become debilitating.

Pedals

While we understand the novice rider's concerns about locking his or her feet into clipless pedal systems, there is no doubt that pedalling efficiency is substantially improved by the adoption of these pedals, developed in the early 1990s. The transmission of power through the cranks and drive train is made massively more efficient with the shoe closely connected to the pedal; some calculations suggest there is an immediate 20 per cent efficiency gain with clipless systems.

We would recommend that the sportive novice adopts clipless technology from the outset. Your initial ride using them may be daunting and could possibly end with the inevitable topple over as you forget to unclip (a rite of passage for any rider…) but they will become second nature within a couple of rides.

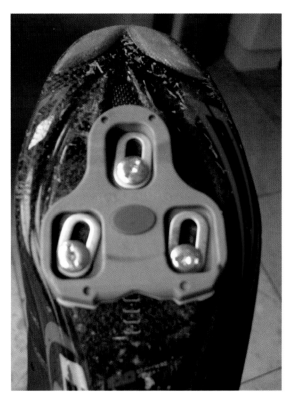

Cleat for a clipless pedal.

A modern-day clipless pedal.

There are various manufacturers and styles out there; choose one of the leading variants, and start with the pedals and cleats (the piece that bolts to the sole of the shoe) at their loosest setting. Most systems allow the rider to adjust the tension of the cleat/pedal fixture, and often also provide different levels of 'float' (an amount of sideways movement in the pedal and cleat). We recommend using cleats with a reasonable degree of float for long events, as this will reduce strain on the knees in particular, and help to minimize injuries. We typically ride with a 9-degree float, which allows movement without feeling slack.

Pedal/Cleat Fit

It is absolutely essential to get the positioning of the cleat on the sole of the shoe correct otherwise repetitive strain and other injuries will almost certainly occur. Only experience will speed up this process, and first of all it is necessary for the rider to follow some basic steps to get the set-up right.

There are several key elements to the positioning of cleats on shoes: first is the forward/ backward location, where the ball of the foot should be more or less directly over the centre of the pedal axle – although this will vary slightly depending on foot size. In general terms, bigger feet will need the cleat set back a little, and the opposite for smaller feet. You will need to experiment, as cleat positioning is highly individual and is also related to how you pedal. For example, a rider with a slightly more 'forward' position will often have the cleats forward on the shoe, as this engages the quadricep muscles strongly. Conversely, setting cleats further back will assist in utilizing the largest muscle set, the gluteal muscles.

Second is rotational positioning: while in theory it may be best to have the feet pointing directly forward parallel with the bike, not all riders are able to achieve this. Legs and feet are as individual as the rest of our bodies, and you may well find that one or both feet naturally point outwards or inwards, or your knees may do the same. In addition to using cleats with a certain amount of float, it is necessary to position them to achieve the optimum balance between comfort, efficiency and power. A very small lateral adjustment can make a big difference.

There are various ways of working out what is the best position for you, but we would suggest that you start by sitting on a kitchen table or bench and allowing your feet to hang loosely, keeping hips, knees and ankles at 90-degree angles. Look down and note the way your feet are pointing, and start by setting your cleat position to reproduce this when you are on the bike. Remember, if you rotate the front of the cleat towards the outside edge of the shoe, the foot position will rotate inwards towards the cranks, and vice versa. You would be amazed how many cyclists never seem to get the hang of that. And remember, an adjustment of even a millimetre or two will induce a big change in foot position.

Once you have set the cleats in what you think is the correct position, take a short spin, carrying an allen key with you, and make adjustments until you find the exact position for your anatomy. Once this is complete, then mark the location by using an indelible marker to trace round the perimeter of the cleat on the bottom of the shoe, so that when changing cleats you can simply place the new one inside the silhouette of the old cleat. Check cleats regularly, and replace them when the front clip-in section becomes worn. At the start of every ride check that the cleat bolts are secure.

For the best advice available on pedal/cleat fit and all other aspects of bike fit, we would recommend Andy Pruitt's great book *Complete Medical Guide for Cyclists*, published by Velo Press. This is the most comprehensive guide to bike fit and injury prevention we have found, besides providing a host of other useful information.

The Importance of Bike Fit

It is essential that a bike fits properly to optimize performance and to reduce the chance of injury. Nor is it enjoyable to ride a machine that is simply the wrong size or set-up, and in a long event such as a sportive, 'repetitive strain'

HELMETS

The argument still rages as to whether cycling helmets do or do not reduce injuries caused in accidents and collisions. We have our own strong views and never ride without a helmet, although the argument is irrelevant in the context of sportives, as all organizers stipulate that the wearing of a helmet is compulsory. All modern helmets are required to meet the EN 1078 Safety Standard published in 1997, and this forms the basis of the British Standard BS en 1078:1997. Compliance with, or exceeding this standard is essential for modern helmets, so make sure that you check the numbers when you buy one, especially if it is made outside the European Union.

---

niggles and injuries are common enough anyway, without making things worse. A bike that is too big or too small will cause over-reaching or shortening of the riding position, both of which will lead to neck, back and other pain and possibly injury.

Every rider has a different anatomy, and to a degree every rider will vary their position from the theoretically 'correct' position for their shape and flexibility. But it makes sense to start from the right place and then to make adjustments to suit, based on experience and preference, whilst also being aware of the impact and effect of adjustments. The authors are constantly amazed in discussions with experienced, regular sportive riders and other high-mileage riders when we realize that they know very little about bike fit and position on the bike, and we often have to overcome the temptation to stop other riders and offer advice on the topic.

Beyond the basic point that the bike itself must be the right size and specification for the type of event for which it is bought, then the fit around the major 'contact points' – the saddle, handlebars and pedals – is what makes the crucial difference for comfort and performance.

Bike and Frame Sizing

Frames come in all sizes, and in a surprisingly wide range of geometries. The key metrics, as we have said earlier, revolve around the seat and top tube length and the angles of the frame geometry. A sportive bike will have more 'relaxed' angles than an all-out race bike, for example. But many sportive riders will buy a complete package from a known manufacturer, and the basic decisions will have been made. So what is critical is that the size of the frame is right for the individual.

A word of caution here: frames also come in different shapes, namely traditional or sloping, and these variations, along with the different ways that different manufacturers and bike builders measure their frames, means that the stated size therefore varies significantly from one machine to another.

Sloping and 'traditional' top tubes.

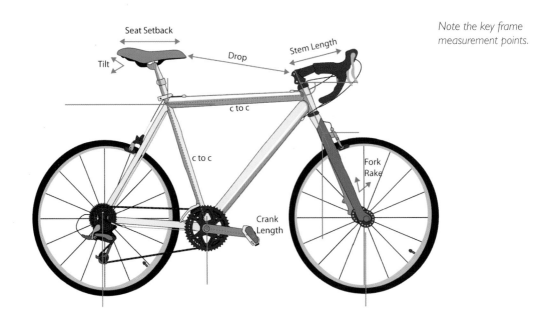

Note the key frame measurement points.

A 'sloping' top tube frame, size 52cm, for example, probably equates to a 'traditional' (horizontal) 56cm, give or take a centimetre or two. So establish what type of frame you are looking at, and work from there.

Frames are often and confusingly measured from different points, but hopefully and increasingly in general terms the key measurements should be consistent between manufacturers, and should be taken 'centre to centre' from the joint areas of the frame itself. In the case of the seat tube, the length will be taken from the centre of the frame where the seat tube and the top tube meet, down to the centre of the bottom bracket. For the top tube, check the measurement from the centre of the joint where the head tube meets the top tube, to the centre of the joint where the top tube meets the seat tube.

When buying a bike it is important to get these reference points right; a variance of a couple of centimetres makes a big difference to bike fit. We are not saying that a given rider can't ride bikes of slightly different dimensions, because personal flexibility and adaptability will allow some people some leeway; for example, one of us (BJ) has 52cm sloping frames through to 57cm traditional framed bikes with differing geometries and significantly different saddle/handlebar drops,

but his flexibility in the lower back area allows him to adjust quite comfortably to different positions.

Other important measurement elements include handlebar stem length and crank arm length. These are often overlooked, or their importance is diminished in the overall scheme of things, but in fact these details dictate some critical elements of your position on the bike, including reach and leg length.

The width of the handlebars is also important, as this will influence the position ('open' or 'closed') of the rider's chest while riding, and thus influence breathing and oxygen uptake. Remember also that the wider the bars, the farther apart the arms will be, and the more the body will be pulled forwards, which may not suit smaller or lighter riders, including women. The general guideline is that the width of the bars should be the same as the width of the rider's shoulders, give or take a centimetre, when measured centre to centre of the bars. Handlebars sometimes incorporate a flat-top central section, which many riders find comfortable on long climbs when riding with their hands on the bars. Hook shapes also vary, with a modern bar often having a flat 'ergo' section, which makes riding down 'on the drops' more comfortable.

Handlebar width should be the same as your shoulder width.

Try out different styles of bar until you find one which suits you. As a useful guideline, if you have the correct head tube height and bar height, your knees will be between 2.5 and 5cm from your elbows at the top of the pedal stroke.

Finally, of the core measurements, the relative height of the saddle and handlebars is crucial to comfort over a long-distance event. Too steep a drop to the bars and the rider will almost certainly suffer neck pain, too little drop causes greater wind resistance, and therefore burns more energy. Power output can also be affected by the depth of the drop, with many riders actually pushing out greater wattage when they sit slightly more upright. In general terms, when setting up the bike, use the following guidelines:

- Off the bike, if you struggle to touch the floor with your fingertips when bending down with the legs straight, then set the handlebars at the same height as the saddle
- If you can touch the floor with your fingers splayed out, then set the bar height between 5 to 10cm lower than the saddle
- If you can stand with your palms flat on the floor without discomfort, then it is possible you may be able to adopt the 'pro' rider's position and set the bars 10 to 15cm lower than the saddle.

The reach to the handlebars on a road or sportive bike is one of the dominant dimensions; the total reach of the rider from the saddle to the handlebars is called the virtual top tube length. Make sure that the top tube of your chosen bike allows you to achieve the optimum reach. (If you have the correct reach you will find that when looking down you will be unable to see the front hub as it will be obscured from view beneath the handlebars while riding on the drops.)

Basically, a shorter rider (up to about 170cm) will need a top tube length of up to 52cm or 54cm, a medium to tall rider (up to about 182cm in height) will need 54cm or 56cm and a tall rider of 183cm and above will look for 56cm or 58cm upwards.

The final adjustment can be made via the handlebar stem, which connects the handlebar to the bike. These can vary in length from as short as 80mm, and as long as 140mm. In general, the shorter the stem the more 'direct' the steering will feel, and the more upright the rider will be. Our advice would be to make sure the frame size and top tube dimensions are correct, rather than trying to make the bike fit through a longer or shorter stem.

OPPOSITE: A relaxed and comfortable position.

Getting Help With Bike Fit

Our intention is not to make the reader spend his or her hard-earned cash unnecessarily, but we do feel that for the serious sportive rider, expenditure on a proper bike-fitting session is a good investment. A good cycle shop should offer at least a rudimentary bike-fitting service, and we would argue that any good, professional outfit would have at least a basic 'jig' or even a software package that gives the buyer a set of measurements to take away, and which serves as a reference point for the future.

It really isn't enough for the bike salesman to take your money, adjust the bar height and wave goodbye. What happens when you pack the bike for an overseas event, or change the saddle, or upgrade the group set, and then need to rebuild it exactly to your specification? So you need the basic data of your own specific bike measurements along with the bike itself. And it isn't always enough to work from 'typical' values, as human dimensions vary greatly.

For example, by reference to one of us again: BJ is a shade under 6ft tall, with an inside leg measurement of 31.5in. Typically he rides a 56cm frame bike, and has a seat tube/leg riding length of 75cm from the top of the saddle to the centre of the bottom bracket. One of his regular training partners, Simon, is identical in height, but has a 33in inside leg and has a seat tube/leg riding length of almost 79cm. All their other key measurement points are equally different. If BJ rode Simon's bike for any length of time, it could well result in an over-extension leg injury and a loss of power output, and the other way round would cause excessive strain on Simon's quad muscles and discomfort in the lower back area. In neither configuration would the riders achieve optimum power output or comfort, resulting in sub-optimal performances, pain and eventual injury.

So it matters, therefore, to make sure that you either get a bike-fit session as part of the overall purchase package, or spend the money to get a full fitting done. And as mentioned above, it is also recommended that you buy a copy of Andy Pruitt's book, as it offers the best and most straightforward advice on all aspects of bike fit.

No matter which type of frame you buy, the measurements of the contact points (the points at which the human makes connection with the bike) should end up the same, although the look of the machine will be very different between traditional, sloping and compact frames.

Remember that when you actually ride the bike you are constantly shifting position. As you pedal, you rise slightly in the saddle, and therefore any adjustments you make while static will result in a different saddle height than if the same measurements were made during a ride. That goes for reach as well: as your effort increases, your hamstrings and lower back muscles tighten, creating the effect that the bars are further away. So for the first few rides after buying a new machine, take some allen keys and make the necessary micro-adjustments to get the fit absolutely right.

The Overall Balance

Achieving the 'right' fit at all the contact points is important, but once the set-up has been completed, ask an experienced cycling friend or a cycling shop to take a look at the overall balance of the bike and its components. The look and feel of the complete bike should be 'right' as well – the drop from saddle to the bars, the reach to the handlebars, the length of the stem in relation to the top tube, the length of seat post in relation to the length of the seat tube, and so on. The bicycle is a beautifully balanced and poised machine, and something which is out of synchronization with its fellow components or indeed its rider will be obvious to an experienced and knowledgeable cyclist.

The end result should look balanced and in proportion. Don't try to compensate for a badly fitting frame with, for example, extra long or extra short components, unless you have a specific physiological reason for doing so.

Similarly, if you are seated on a bike that fits well, you shouldn't experience muscular or physical stress and strain as soon as you reach for the drops on the handlebars, and

you should be able to rest on the tops of the bars with arms very slightly bent and the back at an angle of around 45 degrees. You are not a pro rider who will typically achieve an almost horizontal back position without any apparent effort. These riders have spent thousands of hours training their bodies to ride in those positions; they do stretching and flexibility work to allow them to achieve it, and they are, dare we say it, often considerably younger than many average sportive enthusiasts. One main reason they adopt these relatively extreme positions, apart from increased aerodynamic efficiency, is to lower their centre of gravity, which helps them corner and handle the bike so impressively.

From your more practical and comfortable position, make sure you can reach and operate the brakes without excessive stretching and straining, and just move around and test everything until you know you have the set-up right. Remember that as you ride you will need to shift around on the bike and saddle to change your posture for flat sections or climbs; make sure you can do this easily and comfortably without loss of control.

Of course you will make adjustments over the months and years as your body, your riding position and physique change, but keep the basic reference measurements and use these as the start point. Interestingly, Eddie Merckx made constant adjustments to his bike – sometimes during a race – all through his career, as he was never comfortable with his set-up. In his case it was found to be the result of physiological characteristics and differing leg lengths, so while one side was comfortable, the other wasn't. Toward the end of his career it was said that his mechanics were instructed to keep tools away from him so that he couldn't make adjustments as he rode!

Establishing Bike Fit Yourself

Not everyone will have the luxury of a professional bike fit, so if you find yourself in the position of owning a bike without knowing your specific measurements, here's what to do:

Adjusting Saddle Height and Position
The correct saddle position should enable the rider to deliver maximum power through each pedal stroke. The knee should not be over-extended or 'locked out' (dead straight) at the end of the stroke, and the overall stroke should look and feel smooth and circular.

To get a close approximation of the correct measurement for you, simply multiply your inside leg measurement by 110 per cent, and use this as the distance between the top of your saddle and the top of the pedal at full extension.

Leg position at the bottom of the pedal stroke.

On the bike when pedalling, your leg should be extended at the bottom of the pedal stroke to about 95 per cent of straight, and your hips and pelvis should remain steady without rocking from side to side when pedalling with some effort or at high revolutions (cadence). Your foot should finish the pedal stroke slightly toe-down to the ground. There is much debate about 'ankling', as it is known, but if you observe the riders with the most fluent styles, they tend to follow this distinct pedalling pattern instinctively. These riders have what is called in professional circles '*la supplesse*'.

As we train and compete in events we regularly notice riders whose leg position on the bike is just plain wrong, with hips rolling and rocking from side to side with every pedal stroke, or legs barely straightened even at the bottom of the motion.

Unless an expert has given you a good reason otherwise, set the saddle at horizontal to the ground, using a spirit level to get it absolutely right if necessary. If, after riding with the saddle completely horizontal, you feel you are uncomfortable, then perhaps adjust the tilt of the saddle so that the 'nose' is raised a fraction. If you are a male rider this will have the added advantage of taking pressure off your sensitive areas. Time Triallists will be the only main exception to that rule, as they often ride with the nose tilted slightly downwards to achieve a more aggressive position with the quadricep muscles being brought more into play to achieve more power on the flatter courses.

Establishing the Right Saddle Position

With your leg engaged in the pedal cleat, raise your leg to the top of the pedal stroke. Then get a friend to drop a line from the point of your kneecap, and see where this dissects the pedal. The line should drop directly through the centre of the pedal, or the 'spindle' as it is called. If it is significantly in front of or behind that point, then the saddle needs to be moved forwards or backwards to achieve this position.

Many riders have legs and knees that don't achieve a smooth, vertically rising upwards and downwards, flowing, circular motion while pedalling, including some who are very strong and capable. If this applies to you, there may be nothing that can be done about this, but just check that it isn't caused by specific issues with foot arches or other structural/ physiological problems. If it is, then sometimes custom insoles or specific shoes may help. These 'orthotics' can either be sourced from a specialist, or in some cases from the top bike shops with full fitting facilities.

Remember that any movement of the leg to the side or away from a direct, linear up-and-down flow will displace and therefore waste valuable energy. It may also lead to repetitive strain injury over time.

The ball of your foot should be positioned directly over the pedal spindle, so adjust your shoe cleats to achieve this once the saddle is in the right position. In general, the foot whilst locked into the cleat should be more or less pointing straight forward. Some riders will need to turn their shoes in or out slightly to suit their individual anatomy. It takes

Setting the correct saddle position.

time to get the precise cleat positioning right; as we said earlier, for the first few rides with new pedals or cleats, take an allen key or small screwdriver to be able to make fine adjustments to the location of the cleats.

Positioning the Handlebars/Brake Hoods

The location of the brakes and hoods in relation to the handlebar drops will vary from rider to rider, but make sure above all that when 'on the drops' you can reach and operate the brakes comfortably and without undue effort and strain. Ideally you should be able to do this with a single finger, although as long as it takes no more than two, that's ok.

Start by positioning the top of the hoods more or less on the horizontal, but check that this creates a comfortable reach position. Some riders will position the hoods slightly higher up the bars than this, or will twist the bars to raise the hoods, but go too far and you will create strain through the wrists, and up into the neck on a long ride. The lower the handlebars in relation to the saddle, the more extension load will be placed on the neck when you look forward over the bars.

ABOVE: *Make sure your fingers can reach the levers on the drops.*

LEFT: *Example of bars positioned forward to suit rider style.*

- Make sure the key components are in proportion; don't try to make a poorly fitting frame fit by adding an extra long stem
- If second-hand, ask detailed questions, and check that you are using the same measurement points as the seller
- Invest most in the frame, then the wheels, then the groupset
- Specify or fit appropriate tyres for the event conditions, puncture protection and grip being the two most essential elements
- Avoid a large drop from the saddle height to the top of the handle bars unless you are highly flexible in the lower back
- Ensure the frame has fixing points for two bottle cages as you will need to hydrate well during the sportive
- Be aware of the effect of adjustments; a very small increase in saddle height, for example, can cause big changes in power output and comfort.

Experience Says ...

- Have a proper bike-fitting session done, and record the basic measurements
- Give priority to bike fit and geometry rather than weight or materials
- Buy a pre-specified sportive bike package as a first-time buyer
- Buy the right size frame, bearing in mind that you need a more relaxed geometry for long sportive riding

Clothing

A topic that possibly preoccupies most dedicated cyclists more than any other is their wardrobe. It would be impossible to be definitive about what the best, most appropriate or most fashionable cycling apparel is – this is as much about personal taste and, dare we say it, effective marketing as it is about suitability for purpose. Throughout this book we have refrained from specifying individual manufacturers, labels or brands; our own choices are probably indicated in many of the photos we have used, but we both have some items hidden in our cycling wardrobes from almost every garment producer on the planet.

Above all, cycle clothing has to be fit for purpose and has to do its specific job at whatever time of year you are out there training or competing, in an infinitely variable range of climatic conditions. So the approach we intend to take in this section is to identify the basic requirements and illustrate what we would wear for a given set of conditions. Here in the UK that usually means unpredictable and changing weather patterns, and a fair dose of rain, wind and cold. Even in sunnier and drier climes, over the six, seven, ten hours of a major sportive, and especially one in the mountainous areas of Europe, you may well be subjected to a range of weather conditions, so the ability to adapt and be flexible is essential. Modern technical fabrics such as lycra do exactly what they say they do: they are light, aerodynamic, and they offer a wide range of characteristics from wicking moisture away from the skin to maintaining body heat by incorporating thermal fabrics such as Roubaix fleece.

The key with cycle clothing, particularly in the cooler parts of the year, is to ensure the right level of protection against the elements while also controlling body temperature, allowing freedom of movement and remaining flexible and adaptable to changing conditions. For the year-round sportive rider the biggest task for the long months of the training year is to keep the muscles warm and loose to avoid injuries. And a sportive event is likely to start in the cool of the early morning and progress through the warmest part of the day, possibly encountering rain and winds along the way.

Recommended kit for a winter ride.

Cold Weather/Winter Riding (0°C to 5°C)

It is absolutely essential that in the dark, dreary days of winter the rider is fully protected against whatever the weather can throw at him or her; training all year round can be enjoyable, and is necessary for base-building and maintaining/improving aerobic conditioning, but it isn't enjoyable to be cold, wet and miserable halfway round a long, slow base-training session as the sleet drives in on a gale-force wind from the Arctic. However, there is no need for this to happen: modern protective clothing is technically advanced and highly effective – although as we all find out, there is no such thing as 'waterproof' if the deluge is constant and unrelenting and the spray is being driven up by your wheels.

Nevertheless, our sportive riding friends from the north of Norway introduced us to the expression 'there is no such thing as bad weather, just the wrong clothing', and we have had cause to understand what they meant by it on numerous occasions, including a terrifying ride in rain, sleet, ice and snow in the Arctic Circle a couple of years ago.

The picture above shows a typical winter riding outfit, sometimes augmented by various alternatives, but based on the following:

- Helmet, with light fleece skull cap or headband below it.
- Protective glasses with a clear lens
- Thermal base layer – possibly a sleeveless first layer and a second full sleeve layer
- Long bibtights with wind-protective knee sections and fleece/ 'roubaix' lining
- Wind and waterproof thermal (reflective) top

- Winter-weight full finger gloves and thermal liners
- Cycling shoes with winter-weight thermal socks (one pair only to maintain circulation and shoe fit)
- Thermal/waterproof neoprene overshoes.

As far as we are concerned, for winter riding in particular there is no substitute for quality; when conditions are bad, buy the best and most durable you can afford. In addition to the main cycling retail chains, use auction sites such as ebay (www.ebay.co.uk) as they are a very useful source of good quality kit at sensible prices.

Remember also, that if you have to choose, then wet is preferable to cold, so whatever your outer 'shell', make sure that it is windproof and well sealed against the elements.

Spring and Autumn Riding (6°C to 14°C)

Spring and autumn are possibly the most difficult seasons to ride in and get clothing correct; the ride often starts in very chilly conditions and ends in warm sunshine. Our advice is to wear enough to keep the worst of the chill off as you

begin the ride, but be able to remove layers such as gilets or arm/knee warmers as you need to and as your exertions generate heat. A typical outfit for us would look like this:

- Helmet, with light fleece headband or cycling cap if required
- Protective glasses with a light tint
- Thermal/wicking base layer
- Three-quarter bib with light fleece/Roubaix lining
- Long sleeve, high collar, medium weight windproof/ water-repellent jersey with light Roubaix lining
- Medium-weight full-finger gloves
- Medium-weight socks
- Gilet or lightweight wind/rain jacket.

Summer/Warm Weather Riding (15°C upwards)

It is easy to get clothing right if you happen to live on the Costa Del Sol, but even in high summer, North European days can deliver a startling mix of weather and temperature, and as we have said before, many events begin early before the sun has risen very far, and the temperature can be quite low. So make sure you have a lightweight gilet or protective jacket in a pocket; it will be vital for a long descent after a

Recommended kit for spring/autumn.

Recommended kit for a summer ride.

hot, sweaty climb anyway. In the old days the pro riders would grab a newspaper from a spectator and shove it down the front of their race jerseys (and amazingly enough, even in the 2010 Tour de France, numerous riders were grabbing newspapers from spectators for this very purpose). Nowadays, of course, we usually have the luxury of lightweight, high-technology cycling garments, which do the job rather more conveniently and elegantly.

For most summer rides we would recommend the following:

- Helmet with cycling cap underneath to absorb sweat if required
- Dark lens protective glasses
- Lightweight sleeveless wicking base layer
- Lightweight short-sleeve full zip jersey
- Arm warmers/knee warmers
- Bib shorts
- Fingerless mitts with terry cloth pad
- Lightweight socks or shoe liners.

A Few Practical Pointers

A typical sportive will last for anything from six to ten hours. Conditions can and do change dramatically, and with many events taking place in remote or hilly regions, there is every chance of weather patterns altering. So the key strategy is to work out what combination of clothing will allow you to adapt to changing conditions and maintain optimum physical comfort throughout. Most sportives start early, sometimes before the sun has really risen high enough to warm the area, so make sure you wear enough to offer protection while being able to remove layers and keep them handy. We prefer bib shorts, three quarters or longs simply because they offer protection for the vital organs around the midriff and also provide and maintain a better, more precise fit.

But clothing is a very personal choice; these are only guidelines. Remember that you will almost certainly feel chilly at the start of your event, but as you ride and burn energy, thereby generating heat, you will warm up. So start off by feeling cool but not shivering, and you will probably have it about right. It is amazing to think that about 80 per cent of the effort and calories expended while riding is actually lost in heat production; even a super-fit athlete is usually only about 25 per cent 'efficient' when it comes to energy usage as measured by calories consumed and burned. So your body is going to be taking care of the heat situation most of the time, whether you clothe it or not.

Experience Says ...

- Your clothing has to do the job it was bought for, so do the research to make sure it has been tested
- Buy the best you can afford – quality is important
- Modern technical clothing and fabrics work, so use them to improve comfort and performance
- Conditions change, so wear and carry adaptable clothing such as a gilet or lightweight jacket
- Start out cool – you will warm up as the ride progresses
- There is no such thing as waterproof – but warm is more important than dry, so make sure you are protected from the elements
- Use protective glasses with interchangeable lenses
- Wear a sleeveless layer even in hot conditions, to help wick moisture away and maintain body temperature
- Wear bibs to protect vital organs and to maintain their fit as you ride
- Don't cramp your feet in winter – you need circulation to keep warm
- Always carry a gilet or lightweight jacket for descents or wind protection
- Wear several thin layers rather than one thick one.

CHAPTER 3

TRAINING

This book is aimed at those who care about their health and performance, and who understand that in order to achieve something worthwhile they need to invest time and effort. There should be something for every rider here, but there is still a great deal of truth in the old clichés: 'You get out what you put in', 'Effort brings its own reward', and so on. The message is simple: to be the best you can be, and to achieve the result you want in a sportive, you have to 'do the homework' – that is, cover the miles and get the preparation right.

Of course each individual has their own goals, objectives and lifestyle, which will dictate the level and intensity of the training they undertake. In fact first of all, you, as an individual, should plan your activity to match and suit what you need to get out of it. Don't, as some riders do, try to blindly follow the routines and regimes of their heroes, because that road can lead to over-training, possible failure, and almost certain disappointment as you simply won't match the achievement and performance level of your cycling hero or heroine.

The science of cycle training is a complex area and we want to avoid over-complicating things. The aim of this chapter is therefore to give a few simple tips on training, which will put you on the right path for success. There is a large volume of literature on the subject available if you wish to read further, and we recommend the following books as a good starting point: *Serious Cycling*, Edmund R. Burke Ph.D, and *Base Building for Cyclists* by Thomas Chapple.

Goals and Objectives

Clearly 'performance' is a very personal measure – it may be successfully completing your first 100-mile ride, it may mean achieving a Gold standard time in the Étape du Tour, or it may just mean beating your best friend to the top of a climb. Whatever your definition, this section will help you assess where and how you can make a difference, and how to attain the best return for your training time.

Our experience has shown that it is important to set long-, medium- and short-term goals to keep you motivated and wanting to get out on the bike in all weathers. If you cannot visualize your goal then it can be easy to start missing the occasional ride or workout here and there, which could ultimately mean that you miss your goals. And a word of caution: there is no more de-motivating a feeling than to keep entering a training mileage or session 'deficit'

into the training log simply because you have built unrealistic targets and goals into the programme. Don't underplay the objectives, but it is better to achieve or even exceed them, than to beat yourself up for not achieving what you set out to do in a fit of enthusiasm at the start of the planning process.

Joe Friel, the acclaimed mountain bike racer, identifies two elements as important to effective training: *wisdom* – knowing the sport (and yourself) in order to make logical decisions; and *knowledge* – understanding why certain plans will have a positive outcome in terms of performance. It is important to remember that training for a sportive is not just about the physical and mental aspects, but should also include replicating the particular stresses and situations that we know you will encounter over the length of an event.

The Key Principles of Training

Before we look at what it takes to build an effective training plan, there are three general principles that you need to integrate into your everyday training: overload, specificity and regression.

Overload

It is easy to get into the habit of chasing miles and undertaking the same ride day in, day out. If this happens you will soon find that your pattern of improvement will stall as your body simply becomes used to the stresses that you are placing on it, and you no longer try to stretch yourself or your capability beyond your comfort zone.

Improving your fitness is the result of a balance between over-stressing, or 'overloading' your body (through workouts, intervals, weights or long rides), and providing the recovery time and platform for cells to recover and go beyond their previous levels of strength. If the overload is too great or you do not allow enough recovery time, then you are subjecting your body to overtraining and this can result in a loss of form or lack of progression. The key to improving fitness is a gradual and planned increase in overload to allow the body to adapt. This does take a level of rigour, and is one area where the use of a heart rate monitor and detailed training diary can help you avoid falling into a cycle of mediocrity.

Specificity

In the context of sportive riding this principle simply means that there is no substitute for riding your bike. The demands of riding a mountainous sportive dictate that you need to subject your body to the physical stresses that you will encounter in the event. This is not to say that running or pushing weights will not help you, but real performance gains come from a degree of focus. How many times do you hear people say 'I don't like hills' or 'I can't descend'? Well, the truth is that you will only improve in critical areas if you actively decide to address these areas of weakness, and spend time on specific sessions where you work on them. Most cyclists spend too much of their valuable training time reinforcing their strengths, rather than focusing on and minimizing their weaknesses.

Regression

If a period of training is missed, then the body will begin to regress to its original state and you will start to lose fitness. For the average person this period is about a couple of weeks, depending on age and base fitness. Without the continued stress from working out, your body will lose previous gains, and that is why it is important to have a realistic training plan that takes into account work and family commitments. This will allow for planned rest without the feeling of guilt that often goes with not riding your bike. It's tough for all of us who love to be out there riding, but rest and recovery time are also good.

Knowing these principles will better prepare you to plan how you can put together a personal training regime that suits your goals, builds on your strengths, and improves your areas of weakness.

Know Yourself

In order to plan your training the first step is to understand your own body and it capabilities, and the two most common ways of doing this are through monitoring your heart rate or your power. While power meters are becoming more popular, they remain expensive and are often fixed to a single bike, so our advice is to start with a heart rate monitor.

Our recommendation is to use a heart rate monitor to determine your level of effort and help you plan your training plan. These have the advantage of being relatively inexpensive and you can of course use them on any bike. (There is further advice on heart rate monitors later in this chapter.)

Determining your Maximum Heart Rate

In order to train for specific improvements in your perform-

ance it is important to know the five key heart rate zones that most training plans are based upon. Knowing the value of these zones specific to yourself is at the heart of planning an effective training plan, and to maximizing your effective performance in an event.

All zones are calculated from knowing your maximum heart rate (MHR). Just as we all vary in height and body mass, everyone has their own personal maximum heart rate, which is determined by their own genes. Your maximum heart rate also decreases approximately one beat per minute per year of age; thus the average MHR of a teenager, for instance, is 220 beats per minute, but a forty-year-old would be expected to have a MHR of 180 (220–40).

Note also that your maximum heart rate is 'sport specific' – it will vary from one sport to another. For a given rate of oxygen consumption, weight-bearing activities such as running raise the heart rate more than cycling (because part of your weight is supported by the bike). So you cannot use your maximum heart rate from running to plan a cycling training programme without running the risk of overtraining.

A great way of finding your MHR is to visit a coach and undertake specific tests, but that may not be possible within your budget. A more simple DIY approach is as follows:

- Weigh yourself – this should be first thing in the morning on the same day each week
- Check your resting heart rate (hold your wrist and count the beats over a ten second interval and multiply by six)
- Ten minutes into a ride, when you are feeling warmed up, find a flat section of road. Note your heart rate. Ride at maximum effort for one minute and then record your heart rate again. This is your maximum heart rate (MHR).

These figures will become 'markers' against which you can measure your improved fitness over time. The fitter you get, the lower the heart rate reading at the start and end of the minute as your heart becomes more efficient over time.

The Heart Rate Zones

There are five training 'zones' or heart rate ranges. They are based on the increase in heart rate as the oxygen consumption of the exercising muscle increases — clearly the harder you are working, the harder your heart needs to pump blood to support your body. As you move up the hierarchy of training zones, exercise intensity increases, and there is a shift from the use of fat as an energy source for the muscle cell, to carbohydrate (at below 70 per cent MHR fat is burned preferentially). As your MHR is reached, there is a shift in the muscle cell towards anaerobic (without oxygen) metabolism, with increased lactic acid production.

Once you have your maximum heart rate you can calculate your zones based upon the following table:

THE FIVE TRAINING ZONES, OR HEART RATE CHANGES

Zone 1: Recovery Under 65 per cent of maximum heart rate	Recovery days/sessions are very easy training sessions. Possibly used when injured, overtrained or following a sportive or race. Helps the body adapt, repair and rejuvenate
Zone 2: Aerobic Under 65 to 72 per cent of maximum heart rate	Endurance: Long endurance workouts to build and maintain base aerobic endurance fitness. Exercise at a 'conversational pace' perfect for fat burning
Zone 3 73 to 80 per cent of maximum heart rate	The tempo of lactic acid production increases, bringing more of the so-called 'fast twitch' muscles into play. Frequently used at the end of the base training phase before moving up to the build phase
Zone 4 81 to 90 per cent of maximum heart rate	Threshold effort is now maximally aerobic and the energy systems are stressed as anaerobic effort and lactic acid production start to limit how long you can maintain effort. You make big fitness gains in this zone, but must be careful to recover fully after sessions
ZONE 5: Anaerobic 91 to 100 per cent of maximum heart rate	Endurance: Interval training is a must, as you need the recovery period between intense bouts of effort. The blood and muscles are full of lactic acid causing a burning sensation, but the body starts to learn how to cope with, and get rid of, these high levels of lactic acid. Big fitness gains can be made at this level – however, too much training in this zone is frequently the cause of overtraining and exhaustion. Duration at this intensity is measured in seconds, recovery in minutes; effort is explosive, and injury is common There is little use for this sort of training for the average multisport athlete: avoid injury and spend time at the lower zones instead

If you always train at low heart rates, you will develop endurance with no top end speed. Conversely if you train hard most of the time, you will never recover completely, and chronic fatigue will harm your performance. The solution is to mix hard training with easy rides in the proper proportions.

The best approach is to stay below 80 per cent of maximum heart rate (zones 1 to 3) on your easy days to build an aerobic base while allowing day-to-day recovery, and then push above 80 per cent when it is time to go hard to improve your high level performance. Avoid training in the 'no man's land' of 75 to 85 per cent of MHR where it is too difficult to maintain the pace for the long rides needed to build endurance and allow some recovery time, but not hard enough to significantly improve your aerobic performance and increase your lactate threshold.

Resting Heart Rate

Your resting heart rate (RHR) is another indicator of your degree of training (and a marker for moving into an over-trained state). As you train and become fitter over time, your RHR should fall as a result of the increased efficiency of the circulatory system. Your heart will increase the volume of blood pumped per beat, and cells will become more effective at extracting oxygen from your blood.

The RHR for an untrained person can vary between sixty and ninety beats per minute; with training, it is not uncommon to see the RHR fall into the low forties or fifties. Regular monitoring of your resting heart rate in the mornings (before getting up and beginning your daily activities) can be used as a monitor for overtraining. A simple way to spot this is that your heart rate on awakening and before getting out of bed is 10 per cent higher than your personal normal for several consecutive days. This is a clear sign to back off your level of intensity for a week before restarting your training plan.

The Training Year

While you need to split specific rides into goals, it is also important to split your year down into manageable periods into which you arrange different goals. You will find it very difficult to attain and keep your best form over a protracted period – especially as long a period as between May and September, which forms the major part of the sportive season.

As this is the case you may find the following guide a useful benchmark to a typical year in the life of a sportive rider:

A TYPICAL YEAR IN THE LIFE OF A SPORTIVE RIDER

January	Events will start to open for entries – many fill fast. Weather could dictate focus on core strength and cross-training with swimming. But try to get out on the bike at least a couple of times a week
February	Perfect time for a training camp in Spain/ the Canary Islands, or more focused bike time – time to start to work on power and hard interval sessions. Keep steady miles to reduce weight
March	Start to increase the length of rides and look to complete your first 50-mile ride of the year
April	Events available almost every weekend – suggest one for April
May	Try to plan for two events this month – training should be about maintenance of base fitness and specific work on climbing and threshold
June	Two events – wonderful opportunity to explore France, Italy or Spain
July	Peak season as the Tour de France kicks off – Étape du Tour always attracts huge entries
August	Relax and enjoy your holiday – time to think about peaking for final events during September while trying to fit in a ride or two around time with the family
September	Often spectacular weather for sportives in the UK – final chance to capitalize on the fitness achieved through the season
October	Time to book that training camp for early spring – something to look forward to. Review the year and assess your goals for next year
November	Rest – you have achieved your goals so do not be afraid to take a couple of weeks off the bike. Finalize your goals and map out your plan for next year
December	Steady miles maintaining weight and recovering. Watch your diet through the Christmas period and start to pencil in events for next season

Fit For Purpose

The key principles of training and how to vary your activity through the year have been covered: now we can break down the fitness elements that will form the basis for success in training. In our experience the key elements for success are:

- Have the right equipment
- Conduct an honest assessment of your goals and current capability
- Attain a level of base fitness
- Maximize aerobic capacity
- Increase lactate threshold
- Ride economically

- Improve your power-to-weight ratio
- Build strength
- Allow time for recovery.

The Right Equipment

Arguably the most important piece of equipment to help you optimize your training is a heart rate monitor (HRM). These vary in price from £20 to £450 depending on the level of complexity, but even the most basic of watches will be able to measure exercise time, calories burned, and maximum and average heart rate.

More advanced monitors are able to record data which can be downloaded into a training diary on a PC – these do

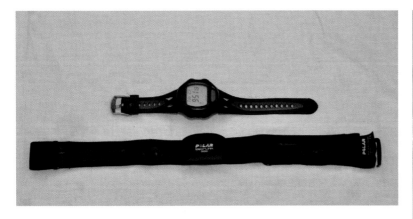

ABOVE: *Heart rate monitor/cycle computer with chest strap.*

RIGHT: *Cycle computer/heart rate monitor mounted on the handlebars.*

provide a valuable aid as you can more easily track your training regime as well as graphically tracking your improvement. Many people are now emphasizing the benefits of power meters as a training aid, and while there is no doubting their effectiveness, a heart rate monitor is more than adequate for the majority of riders training for a sportive.

The second key piece of equipment is a set of digital scales. Your weight is a key determinant in your ability to cycle to your optimum ability; cycling is a sport in which power-to-weight ratio is one of the most critical measures of performance, especially when climbing. It is important to weigh yourself at the same time on the same day, and also not to weigh yourself too often – monitoring your weight once per week should become a key part of your routine, and is a key measure of the success of your training plan.

We have referred to the point elsewhere, but we see

A top-end body composition monitor digital scales.

many riders fussing with miniscule reductions in bike weight while ignoring the obvious potential for their own weight loss and resulting power-to-weight gain. A few kilos of weight loss over a long period of training for a sportive is not an impossible goal, and it takes no more self-discipline than the training plan itself.

The third essential for effective training is clothing (see Chapter 2, page 39, for detailed advice); this is especially true in winter. If you do not have the right clothing to keep you dry and warm, then no amount of willpower is going to get you out on the road.

An Honest Assessment

The start point for any training plan has to be an honest perspective on where you are in terms of fitness, and what your goals are. This assessment will provide the reference point for improvement over time, and will also play a key role in determining the factors that will become an important reference point as you track your progress.

There are several ways of doing this. The most scientific is to visit a coach for a physical assessment of weight, fat content, heart rate, anaerobic threshold, lactate threshold and power. This will cost you over £100 (unless you can get tested for free at a local University Sports Department), but we strongly recommend it, as this information will help enormously in getting the maximum return for the time invested in training. The critical measurements it will give you, so you can ride to your potential, concern the amount of fat you are carrying.

A regular sportive rider prepared to put in the structured training and change their nutritional habits can attain a body fat percentage of between 10 per cent and 18 per cent. Pure power to weight can be drastically enhanced through a reduction in excess body fat. Shedding a modest amount of weight should be an essential part of the overall plan, as it has such a direct impact on your performance.

Assessing Your Lactate Anaerobic Threshold

In simple terms this is the maximum effort at which your body can operate without building up excess lactate in your blood, causing you to back off your effort to allow your body to recover. It is important to know this threshold as it also tells you at what level you start burning more precious carbohydrates than fat. Even the thinnest people carry many thousands of calories of energy in fat but can only carry a small amount of carbohydrate energy (glycogen). Therefore the further and harder you can ride burning fat, the better your ability to ride faster and farther without running out of fuel and encountering the dreaded 'bonk'. This is where 'base training' really helps to teach your body to burn fat at higher levels, and earlier on in the ride.

Assessing VO$_2$ Max

VO$_2$ max is a measure of your aerobic capacity, and is the maximum amount of oxygen which your body is able to transport to the working areas of the body. Oxygen is used in the aerobic processes of energy production within cells. Your body uses oxygen at a low rate at rest, at a faster rate as you begin to exercise, and reaches its fastest rate of oxygen consumption near your maximum heart rate. The more oxygen that the body can effectively transport and utilize, the higher a person's VO$_2$ max, and the greater their potential, other key factors all being equal.

The maximum amount of oxygen consumed while an individual is working their hardest produces an excellent indicator of cardio-respiratory fitness. For endurance athletes, a higher VO$_2$ max indicates a higher potential for endurance performance. Greg Lemond, Tour de France winner, had one of the highest ever recorded VO$_2$ max values at ninety-two (an average adult male of forty years old is typically around forty, and a trained sportive rider may well register anything between fifty and seventy).

Assessing Power Output

A coach will look at your power output against heart rate. Power output is measured in watts, and it gives a very good guide as to the strength of the rider. Larger riders will normally have a larger power output than smaller riders, but of course if you are cycling uphill, a larger rider has more weight to drag up the hill so the power advantage is cancelled out. That is why you hear many coaches talking about watts per kilo as a measure of a rider's real power output, and most pro riders focus on this when monitoring their training progress.

To calculate watts per kilo value, divide bodyweight by the maximum watts you can sustain for a set period – for most of us this will mean a visit to a testing lab. Tour de France riders are typically 5.5 to 6.5 watts/kilo, but anything over 4 watts/kilo for an amateur cyclist will put the rider in very good shape to complete a sportive in good time.

With the above information you have a very good understanding of how fit you are and what you need to work on, and you can plan your training accordingly.

Attaining a Level of Base Fitness

Base training fitness is all about building up your body to work at higher levels for longer, which is what endurance athletes need to do to achieve faster times. If you are new to endurance events, it is likely you will need to start your training by doing quite a bit of base training to build up your stamina. The good news about this is that base training doesn't require you to hurt yourself or push hard – rather the opposite.

Base training is all about training at moderate rather than at high levels of effort. Referring back to our zone chart, level 2 is the appropriate zone here, incorporating longer, slower, lower intensity rides of three or more hours if possible.

In terms of sportives, the first goal should be to build up to ride for longer than two hours without feeling tiredness, pain or discomfort. Once this is attained you can easily build towards a 100-mile ride with confidence. This base fitness will come from a gradual build-up of rides starting at 10 miles, then rising over a four-week period to 20, 30 and then 40 miles. As your fitness improves and you spend more time on your bike you will gain confidence and learn the essential elements of hydration, nutrition and road sense. This training can be undertaken on your own or with a friend, but it is important to ride within your limits and at your own pace.

Maximize Your Aerobic Capacity

In terms of sportives, the higher your VO$_2$ max the longer you will be able to ride at a high pace as your body is more efficient at processing oxygen. While it is generally accepted that your capacity is fundamentally predetermined by genetics, personal experience has shown that structured training can result in worthwhile improvements in base values, which have a direct impact on the rider's ability to perform over long distance events.

The good news regarding VO$_2$ max is that it can be improved within certain limits relatively quickly through short intensive sessions – the following exercise has been shown to give as much as a 10 per cent increase in VO$_2$ max after just six weeks:

The four-minute, very intensive mid-section of this exercise will boost both anaerobic and aerobic power and only needs to be completed once per session – the rest of the ride should be at medium intensity. You can also apply the same workout during a run, a swim or at the gym using exercises such as squat thrusts, star jumps and press-ups.

Warm-up	15 to 20 minutes at a steady pace
Sprint flat out	20 seconds
Rest	10 seconds
Repeat	× 8
Warm-down	20 minutes at a steady pace

An alternative VO_2 max work-out is as follows (it is best done on a slight incline):

10min	warm-up, building from easy to moderate
5min	recovery
5min	max effort
5min	recovery
5min	max effort
5min	recovery
5min	max effort
5min	recovery
5min	max effort
5min	recovery
10min	warm-down.

The final maximum power effort should be kept within 10 per cent of the effort of the first one.

Increase Your Lactate Threshold

Although most cyclists refer to lactic acid as the cause of pain or a burning sensation after intense effort, it is actually the release of positively charged protons that is the cause of the problem, and it is the body's ability to clear both protons and lactic acid that is developed during lactate threshold training. The objective here is to 'lift' the anaerobic threshold by stretching your limits to teach your body how to deal with excess lactate accumulation and make it more efficient in metabolizing increased blood lactate levels. Increasing the anaerobic threshold will result in a wider aerobic zone, which allows you to go faster, feel stronger and ride farther before reaching your limit.

Anaerobic workouts must be approached with well directed training strategies as they require specific physical preparation in order to produce the best results in performance. Interval training is not simply interval training: it is a highly effective quality workout when applied at the right time and in the right amounts.

Ride Economically

One of the key determinants of success in a long sportive is your ability to use less energy to produce the same or greater power over the entirety of the event. There are many aspects to 'economy', including low body mass, psychological stress, low frontal area, good posture, strong core muscles and minimizing movement, but whichever is most important, through training you can improve your ability to channel and utilize energy more effectively and efficiently.

Too many times we see cyclists hurtle off in events pushing a high gear, failing to pace themselves, missing food stops and showing poor technique. It is possible, in shorter events, to get away with these bad habits, but ultimately the rider will not be able to maintain good form and pace in the latter stages of a tough, longer event.

Improve Your Power-To-Weight Ratio

There are clearly two important elements in this equation: managing your weight, and improving your muscular strength. Later in the book we outline how nutritional awareness and the right diet can help you reduce and then maintain the correct weight for your physique (see Chapter 5). From a training perspective you need to be very specific with regard to sessions designed to optimize fat burn/weight loss and those designed to increase your power. During these weight-loss or fat-burning sessions you must remain within the specific thresholds you have defined as your fat-burning/aerobic zones. If you move outside these and go 'anaerobic', the human metabolism takes a while to 're-set', and the effectiveness of the session is dramatically reduced.

In our view, the most frequent training mistake we see in novice and even experienced riders is that they try too hard and work outside the optimum zone. The good news is that what is required here is 'LSD' – long slow distance rather than tearing around with high heart rates and heaving chests.

The Holy Grail – Losing Weight

Weight loss is probably the most talked about topic within cycling, referring both to the bike and equipment and the individual who rides it. Cyclists often have an unhealthy obsession with weight reduction, which places them at risk of contracting illnesses and damaging their long-term wellbeing. Yes, power-to-weight is one of the most important factors in riding faster and more strongly, but an obsessive drive to shed every last gram of fat will compromise the immune system and probably result in lost days through illness and infection. Pro cyclists do get down to the absolute minimum levels of body fat, but are often acutely susceptible to catching low-grade infections, and are usually paranoid about protecting themselves from illness.

The average sportive rider is unlikely to subject themselves to a regime and lifestyle designed to reach 3 or 4 per cent body-fat levels as the pros do, and would almost certainly inflict long-lasting negative side effects on their bodies if they did. So the aim must be to reach a sensible and sustainable body fat percentage that takes account of life in the 'real world'.

Body fat percentage will vary from one individual to another, and will to a large extent be governed by physiological 'type', plus dietary factors, metabolism, levels of physical activity and eating patterns. But there are guidelines, and as a very general rule an enthusiastic and committed male sportive rider might aspire to a body fat range of 10 to 18 per cent, while his female counterpart might work within a range of 14 to 22 per cent. Women generally, in physiological terms, have a higher body fat content than men. Average body fat levels amongst fairly healthy and active individuals might range between 14 and 22 per cent for males, and 16 and 26 per cent for females.

As an alternative to looking at absolute body fat level percentages, we also use body mass index measurement, or 'BMI', as this also provides a useful guide to overall fitness and wellbeing. It is BMI that medical practitioners will use to assess an individual's likelihood of heart and other diseases, but it has applicability to athletes as well.

If you are interested in riding a bike to your maximum ability, your objective should be to achieve your optimum power-to-weight ratio, and your body fat level, or body mass index, should be something you are aware of and aim to reduce through your training regime. A reduction of a couple of per cent alongside an increase in power through specific training will reap immediate and very noticeable performance improvements.

There are various ways of calculating body fat percentages, with callipers being one of the most accurate; your own GP can often perform this measure for you, and a local health and leisure centre should also be equipped to do the job. As we have said, many people also use body mass index as a key indicator, and this is straightforward to measure yourself: your weight in kilograms is divided by the square of your height in metres. So for example, an average fit male cyclist weighing 75kg and 1.8m tall would calculate his BMI as follows:

$$1.8 \times 1.8 = 3.24$$
$$75 \div 3.24 = \text{BMI of } 23.15.$$

Broadly speaking, a BMI of below twenty is excellent, and is associated with extremely fit individuals considered to carry a very low risk of conditions such as high blood pressure, heart disease and diabetes, whereas thirty or above is considered obese and to carry a very high risk of such conditions.

But let us say loud and clear that percentage body fat or BMI calculations are not the only key determinants of sportive performance. Of the two authors of this book, it is the one with higher body fat (14 per cent versus 9 per cent) that is the better performer – a bigger aerobic 'engine', higher VO2 max, lower overall bodyweight and stronger leg muscles lead to a higher power output and a faster rider.

So body fat and weight loss should not be seen as the exclusive 'Holy Grail' in the pursuit of enhanced performance. Nutrition, appropriate and specific training, and the right mental approach are all part of the mix. Weight loss should be gradual, to a sensible level, and then sustained through a balanced diet and regular exercise and training regime. Never crash diet, and don't become a slave to body fat reduction. There is no point in ruining the enjoyment of the rest of your life just to knock a few minutes off your next sportive. None of us are about to challenge a Tour de France rider for the top podium spot on the Champs Élysées, so keep it in perspective.

Finally, notwithstanding the previous point, do plan to shed a few grams or kilos of excess weight rather than spend a fortune on the lightest components for the bike. And remember, weight loss is about planning a nutritional programme that meets your training needs as well as being enjoyable, and whilst out there riding, using long, slow distance rides to drive down body fat levels.

Increasing Power

We have spent a while discussing training regimes and weight reduction, which is one part of the power-to-weight equation. The second part is of course power output, and if this can be increased alongside gradual weight loss, the effects will be significant. It stands to reason that within certain limits, bigger muscles will drive more power, which will improve performance. So incorporate into your routine some sessions that are specifically aimed at increasing power.

The following exercise is designed to increase your strength and endurance whilst climbing, and should be completed twice per week:

10min – low-level warm-up, go through gears, elevate heart rate slightly
10min – 65 per cent max HR – moderate effort
10min – 70 per cent max HR – moderately hard effort
10min – 75 per cent max HR – hard effort
10min - 80 per cent max HR – very hard effort
10min – 75 per cent max HR – hard effort
10min – 70 per cent max HR – moderately hard effort
10min – 65 per cent max HR – moderate effort
5min – spin finish.

Building General Strength

Strong muscles are very important in any form of sport, and this is especially true in endurance events. While it is good to get in the saddle and get plenty of miles 'under the belt' (this form of training cannot be replaced), it is also important to use other techniques to give you that edge in the saddle.

Core Strengthening Exercises

Your core is basically the area around your midriff, all the way round. So it incorporates the muscle groups at the front, sides and back of your trunk below the chest and above the buttocks. It is important to note that core strength is derived from the inter-operation between a range of muscles, and there are therefore multiple exercises that can deliver improvement to all these areas.

A strong core is vital to good performance over a sportive. Below are some simple core strengthening exercises that will help you achieve great efficiency of energy, power and comfort on the bike.

It is important that you work on your core only a couple of times a week. Resting between sessions is important to help the muscle recover and develop. Do not over-tense your abdominal muscles; remember that you are building them for endurance, after all. Breathe normally throughout the exercises; holding your breath is a sign that you are not relaxed properly.

The plank.

Superman

Start with hands and knees on the floor. Make sure you keep your back straight. Raise one arm out in front of you. Raise the opposite leg out behind you. Make sure both limbs are straight – it does take some practice to perfect your balance, but bear with it and as your strength improves it will become easier. Hold for thirty seconds. Repeat with the opposite limbs. Perform ten repetitions.

The Plank

The starting position should be similar to that of a press-up. Drop down on to your elbows, being sure that they are directly below your shoulders. Raise yourself on to your toes. Make sure that your legs and back are in a straight line. Balance on your toes and elbows for one minute. Repeat three times.

The superman.

The Side Plank

On your side, make sure that your elbow is directly below your shoulder. Straighten your legs so they form a straight line with your torso. Hold that pose for one minute. Repeat on the opposite side.

The side plank.

Crunches

Lie on your back with your feet flat on the floor and your knees bent. Using your abdominal muscles, raise your shoulders slightly off the ground. Hold for a second, then return the shoulders to the floor. Try to do thirty repetitions. Rest, then repeat.

Crunches.

Gym ball crunch.

An alternative abdominal muscle exercise – target the abdominal side muscles.

Gym Ball Crunch

The crunch can also be performed on a gym ball; this allows you to extend the back further, stretching the abdominal muscles.

Exercise for the Abdominal Side Muscles

This exercise targets the side muscles of the abdomen. Lie sideways on the gym ball. Make sure your pelvis is supporting your weight on the ball. Keep your feet together and form a straight line with your body. Place your hands up next to your head with your elbows bent. Flexing just from the waist, bring your upper elbow down towards your pelvis. Hold for a few seconds. Return to the starting position. Repeat fifteen times. Perform the same exercise lying on the other side.

Leg Raises

Lie on your back with straight legs. Keeping your lower back flat on the floor, raise both heels off the ground approximately 10cm (4in). Hold for 30 seconds. Do not allow your back to become arched.

Leg raise.

Back Extensions

The starting position is face down. Keeping your pelvis on the floor, slowly raise your torso. Hold for 30 seconds.

Back extensions.

Other Strengthening Exercises

The exercises described here are to strengthen the main muscles required in cycling. With most exercises there are at least two options, one using weights and one without. This means you can perform the exercises at home, but if you are a member of a gym, most of them can be performed on dedicated machines. When performing exercises with weights, start with a very light weight and gradually increase it over time.

As an important aside, what is also emerging from the latest research is that cycling, whilst right at the very top of health-sustaining activities, does not improve bone mineral density (BMD) – critical in the maintenance of healthy bones into old age, and essential for the prevention of conditions such as osteoporosis. Recent research has in fact shown that at the extreme end of the sport, pro cyclists could even have up to 10 per cent lower BMD than the average person, putting them at greater risk of bone problems in later life. The reason for this is simple: cycling does not induce load-bearing stress through the main joints (apart from when out of the saddle and sprinting or climbing), and it is this load-bearing capability that strengthens bones and leads to increased BMD.

Most modern coaches therefore now incorporate a couple of weights or resistance sessions into the weekly training schedule; some simple exercises such as squats and presses will provide the necessary load-bearing workout. In fact we would like to emphasize that the more mileage you ride, the greater the need to ensure that you do some load-bearing exercise as well, unless you happen to get this from your job or everyday activity.

The following exercises augment specific strength-building routines:

Gluteal Exercise

Start with the hands and knees on the floor. Make sure you keep your back straight. Raise one leg behind until it will go no further. Do not arch your back or rotate the hips. Slowly return the leg to the starting position, and repeat with the opposite leg. Repeat twenty times.

Gluteal exercise.

Quadriceps.

Quadriceps

The starting position is standing straight. Lift a barbell and place it behind your head. Make sure your elbows are directly below your wrists. Keeping your knees directly above your ankles, lower your body by going into the squat position. Try to keep your back as straight as possible. Slowly return to the start position. Repeat ten times. Try to perform three sets.

Alternative Quadriceps

Standing with your back to the wall, place a gym ball at around buttock height. Press yourself against the gym ball, keeping your back as straight as possible. Making sure your knees are above your ankles, slowly go into the squat position. Do this by rolling down the ball. Return to the start position. Perform ten repetitions. Repeat three times.

Calf Raises

Sit on the edge of a bench. Place your toes on a raised surface. Place a barbell across your knees (you can use padding if required). Keep your knees in line with your ankles. Slowly raise your ankles off the ground. Hold for a few seconds, then return to the start position. Perform ten repetitions. Repeat three times.

Calf Raise Variation

Stand straight with a barbell behind your head. Make sure your wrists are directly above your elbows. Gently lift your heels off the ground. Hold for a few seconds, then return to the start position. Perform ten repetitions. Repeat three times.

Alternative quadriceps.

Calf raises.

Triceps

Start by leaning forwards from the waist. Support your body by leaning on a structure. Place a dumb-bell in one hand. The elbow should be flexed with the forearm pointing towards the floor. Keeping the upper arm static, extend the elbow. Return to the starting position. Repeat ten times. Perform the same exercise using the other arm. Try to do three sets.

Alternative calf raises.

Triceps.

Allow Time For Recovery

It is essential in any effective training plan to allow time for recovery, and to ensure that a day's hard effort is followed by an easier session or a rest day. Most of us lead a busy work-life, so often our time off the bike is dictated by external commitments. All too often, however, when time permits it is tempting to just go and ride hard, which may actually be detrimental to achieving the goals set out in the training plan. If you continue to train at a level of intensity without respite you are not giving your body a chance to repair the damage to muscle tissue – a process that is key to building strength. In that sense, and we see it all the time, it is very easy to keep banging out the miles but actually erode, rather than build, fitness and strength.

The final (but no less important) element to recovery is stretching and a planned warm-down after a ride. It is too easy to rush off the bike following a ride, jump into the shower and get on with everyday life. We may stretch a little before we ride – which for most of us really means the internationally accepted standard of 'bend over once, stretch arms in the air, lunge down on to a leg and ready for the off' – but we will actually gain significantly more from a planned cool-down period and stretching following a ride. The best way to ensure this is by planning it into your routine – have a look at the section of this book dealing with flexibility, strength and avoiding common injuries for details of recommended stretches (Chapter 4).

Massage

At last we can address one of the burning questions of cycling, one which is a source of mystery, amusement and ridicule aimed at 'real' cyclists all over the world: to shave or not to shave – that is the question. Quite apart from its aesthetics, the single most important reason for leg shaving is that it helps a masseur to give a better and more effective massage. It also allows road rash injuries to be treated more easily and hygienically, and then finally – all of us 'real' cyclists think it looks better to have suntanned, oiled and shaven legs as we sprint for the finishing line amongst the screaming crowds …

But to return to the role of massage: not everyone can have a personal masseur, and a good deep tissue massage will cost around £40 per session, so it isn't within everyone's budget, either. But if you can do it, then we recommend that you build in at least a few massage treatments into your schedule, as the benefits are numerous.

A good deep tissue or sports massage will help to remove toxins, including lactic acid, from the muscles, and will generally improve the flow and supply of blood and nutrients to the fatigued areas. It will also speed up recovery and facilitate the repair of minor damage such as muscle strains – it won't fix a seriously damaged or torn muscle, but it will aid the natural regeneration process. Nor, almost certainly, will it be a pleasant and relaxing experience: it will hurt most of the time as the masseur explores damaged tissue and probes to clear toxins from the system. But as part of an overall training and recovery regime, massage should be incorporated into your programme.

A Word of Warning

Don't have a deep tissue massage too soon before a major event; the massage itself causes physical 'side effects' as toxins are released into the bloodstream, and the body needs time to remove these toxins and recover from the session. Many sportives do now offer massages at the end of the ride, but these should be relaxing/light sessions to help you unwind from the intense effort of the event. Stay away from alcohol after a deep tissue massage, and let the body cleanse itself naturally. Try to schedule a rest after the massage treatment, and use it as a reflective and calm period of recovery.

Dealing with Lack of Improvement

It can sometimes be very frustrating if you are training hard but do not seem to be gaining in fitness or moving towards the achievement of your goals. This can be for a number of reasons, but essentially they come down to those outlined below. Be aware of them, be honest with yourself, and act early to avoid making the mistakes outlined:

Training inconsistently: It is all well and good putting in the hard miles at the weekend, but this will not make up for consistency of riding across a week. Likewise, a good week of structured training is good, but not if it is followed by three weeks of inactivity. Plan your week, month and year around your goals, and stick to the plan as much as possible.

Not planning your rest: This is a difficult one to balance. However, if you stress your body too much, you risk overloading and losing many of the benefits of your hard work. Research has shown that the body reacts to stress from many different areas of life in the same way – be it work related, physically related or due to other pressures in day-to-day life. If you are trying to do too much then you should read the signs and back off, take stock of what is important, and re-set your recovery goals.

Taking on the wrong fuel: Eating healthily is important as a lifestyle choice in order to lose weight and fuel your activity. In order to maximize the benefit of any particular session you need to eat the right food before, during and after exercise. For hard sessions make sure you take a carbohydrate drink, and after every session drink a protein recovery shake to help your body repair and prepare for the next session.

Your easy rides are too hard: This is perhaps the most common mistake of all, and psychologically tough to control. Most people head out into a training session feeling they have to go hard at it for the whole session, whereas base-building requires that you back off from pushing up towards and into your anaerobic zone. Pushing the pedals too hard negates the benefits of a recovery ride.

Your hard rides are too easy: Many people perceive that their hard efforts are pushing their limits, whereas in fact they are a long way off their thresholds. To increase strength, capability and capacity you really do have to work hard, and that hurts sometimes.

One of the best ways to push your limits is to ride with a small group of cyclists who you know are currently a level above you in terms of experience and fitness. The dynamics of training rides with others means that there will always be opportunities to push yourself, and you will be very surprised at how quickly your fitness, thresholds and bike-handling skills will develop. This aspect of your training may well be where joining the local cycling club can help; most clubs organize weekly or twice-weekly training sessions where a group of riders heads out and works together for the riders' mutual benefit.

Training Camps

We are strong supporters of training camps. The anticipation leading up to the camp, which lasts for months through the winter, the motivation, the camaraderie and the benefit to your fitness at a key time early in the sportive season, all add up to what should be one of the best experiences you can have on a bike.

Training camps, like sportive riders, come in all shapes and guises: they can be as simple as a few friends booking a week away together, through to a package at a spa resort with coaching, testing and seminars. They are mostly timed to help you fit in a solid block of steady riding before the spring, but you can also find ones with specific objectives, such as preparing to ride a European Gran Fondo such as the Étape du Tour, or a major domestic sportive event. The rest of this section has been contributed by John Fegan of Train in Spain, to give the perspective of a training camp organizer:

The concept of the training camp originates from professional cycling, where pre-season get-togethers have been the norm for decades. The camps are set up to bring riders together and encourage team spirit, to try out new

Early season sun can do wonders for your motivation.

Climbs, sun and pain!

equipment, and to get a solid block of training done on good roads and in good weather. It gives riders a chance to gauge their fitness and for the team directors to assess form.

What is good for the pros is also a great idea for amateur cyclists as well, especially those who live in cold, dark and wet places all winter. Trying to maintain a good level of fitness from October through to March has always been a challenge: either you risk life and limb by taking on the elements and road conditions, or you opt for the safer mixture of spinning classes and turbo sessions.

It can, however, be a great source of motivation if you know you are going to get away for a week or two to someplace where the sun shines and the roads are quiet. You would be surprised at how much motivation to train through the winter this gives you.

The Mediterranean is, historically, the part of Europe that enjoys the mildest winters, the most hours of sunshine and

the least amount of rain. It is where the great majority of professional teams heads every winter: in that of 2009–10, the riders from Sky, Astana, Katusha, Radioshack and Quickstep could be found on the Spanish Costa Blanca escaping the worst of the winter weather.

Who goes on a training camp?

Until recently, amateur camps were mostly attended by club riders and League of Veteran Racing Cyclists stalwarts: there has always been a strong club culture of going to Spain or Mallorca to get some early season form in the legs before the race season starts. But now, with the massive increase in the sportive market, there is a whole new class of rider wanting to experience the benefits of warm weather winter training, with a different set of reasons for heading to the sun. A solid block of training in February or March helps build a real foundation for the sportive rider. And say what we like about low-cost flight operators, they have enabled us all to reach year-round cycling destinations on a reasonable budget.

So, ideally, what type of camp should sportive riders be attending? There are certain key questions that you need to be asking:

- When is the best time to go, to help me achieve my objectives?
- Where should I go? (Consider the average weather patterns, the type of terrain you want to ride on, the ease of getting there, the quality of accommodation, and what the area itself is like to be in)
- Do I want to go on an organized camp with guided rides and a daily itinerary, or just go off myself or with a few friends?
- Will the camp be suitable for my level of riding?

Organized training camps

You can find a variety of training camps through the advertisements in the cycling media every week. Some firms are based in the same place all year round, while others operate camps just during the winter season. The camps that the authors use and recommend are organized by 'Train in Spain' (www.traininspain.net), permanently based around the town of Denia on the Costa Blanca, Spain, which is actually about the driest area of Spain through the winter months.

Before booking in, you need to consider and, if necessary, negotiate and agree the aim of the camp with the organizers. For example, you should discuss:

- Is it a base training camp with the focus on long, steady rides, or is it aimed towards race preparation?
- Does it cater for riders of differing abilities? If so, does it have a number of guides so that the riding isn't constantly being halted to wait for people to catch up?
- Is it a week with coaching and skills training, or is it a 'no frills' option?
- What type of climbing and descending is there?
- What distances will be ridden, and at what type of pace?

Good friends, good weather, good base-building.

- Are there options for shorter rides with café stops?
- Are there other things to do if the weather is bad?
- Do the organizers arrange for the rental of bikes if necessary?
- Are there mechanics on hand, or local bike shops nearby?
- Can I bring my family with me?
- Are there different cost options?

Do your research and speak to the organizers – they are generally all bike fanatics with plenty of experience, and it is in their own interest to make sure you attend a camp that meets your own abilities and criteria.

Pre-camp training

Most training camps are going to be based around five or six days of riding, with options of between 65 and 130km riding each day. You have to be realistic here, because if you want to go out and ride 645km in six days during your off season, then you need to prepare for it. Try to build up your mileage progressively in the weeks before the camp. If you don't live near hills, simulate climbs with turbo sessions, and practise group riding whenever possible.

What to take

If you have chosen the Mediterranean as your destination, you still need to keep an eye on the weather beforehand and ask the organizers how it is just before you go. Team Sky chose Valencia for their first Training Camp in 2010 based on it having the mildest and driest weather in Europe. When they arrived they were faced with snow, rain and the coldest winter in decades. So be prepared, it can be wet and windy – it is just less likely than back home. As well as your helmet and shoes, take a wind gilet, a rain jacket, overshoes, gloves, leg and arm warmers as well as enough changes of kit to allow for washing and drying of what you've just worn.

If you are taking your bike rather than renting one, think about the riding you are going to be doing. If it is mostly climbing and descending, then those deep-section carbon wheels aren't going to be your best friends. Likewise, leave the TT aero bars behind – they are considered dangerous in group riding situations. If you have been experimenting with tubular tyres, leave them at home, too, as clinchers are easier to deal with in the event of punctures or damage. Organizers are likely to carry spare inner tubes and maybe tyres as well, but few will carry tubulars, glue or tape in their support vans.

Most importantly, make sure the bike is in good mechanical order. Get down to your local bike shop a week or two before the camp for a service if possible. As a minimum, do the bike and equipment check recommended in the bike handbook.

Eating and drinking

Camps vary from being in self-catering apartments to all-inclusive resorts. Whichever you choose, try to make sure you eat healthily during the week. If you have been on a diet, avoid starving yourself during the week: your body will need more calories than normal if it is to function properly. Ingest a good balance of carbohydrates and protein throughout the day, especially at breakfast time.

Hydration is one of the most overlooked areas amongst sportive riders. We have seen people going out for a five-hour ride with two bidons, and returning with only one used. The routes should have water stops built into them (or have a support vehicle carrying water for you), so make sure you drink plenty. Likewise your body needs a steady intake of energy when you are spending long hours on the bike, normally in the form of bars and gels, fruitcake, bananas and sandwiches. Make sure you eat a little amount at regular intervals to keep your energy levels high.

Camp chumps

Apart from those who arrive without a reasonable level of fitness, the most common behaviour that we encounter as organizers is from people who want to treat the camp as their personal Tour de France. There is nothing wrong with a bit of daily competition, but some riders have a compulsion to prove that they are the fittest and fastest rider in the group, climb after climb, day after day. They want to race with the coaches, the guides, with buses, motorbikes, local pros – whatever moves, they want to beat it. If there is more than one like this, rides become a suffer-fest as they try to rip each other's legs off.

This sort of behaviour is, of course, seen on club rides every week of the year, but it is not good or appropriate in pre-season training. As organizers, we have seen Category 1 riders go home from a camp and take a month to recover because they have burnt themselves out.

If you have picked your camp carefully, as one that caters for your level of riding, then the routes and pace should be manageable – not too easy, not too hard. The idea is that you go home fitter, not needing another holiday to recuperate. If a faster rider finds they are frustrated by the group pace, they can be accommodated by the guides who can provide extra specific work to do such as extra loops, hill repeats and brow sprints to ensure that the more able rider also gets a good workout. But what shouldn't happen is that the faster rider dictates the pace of the group.

Enjoy the camp

Do not overestimate your ability or your fitness level. If you have been training for five hours a week throughout the winter, then tackling twenty hours over a few days is likely to be tough for you. If your muscles are screaming after the first day or two, consider taking a rest day, or ask the organizers for a route that is good for an easy spin.

Let the organizers know if you have specific concerns or areas of weakness that you want to improve. For example:

- You are not used to group riding and 'following wheels'

- You are not familiar with the concept of 'through and off'
- You are nervous about technical descending.

All of this is second nature to club riders, but sportive riders often train alone; then when they are in a peloton, they make moves that are dangerous to themselves and to their fellow riders. Too many crashes are caused by riders braking when there is no need to brake, overtaking other riders on the inside, and crossing the white line on fast descents. Other common mistakes are going to the front of a group to take your turn and inadvertently driving the pace up.

If you are following a personal training plan, accept that when on a camp with other riders the itinerary is not going to be changed just to suit you. Instead, speak with your coach about how best to ensure the week can be built in to your plan.

Take advantage of all the experience of the organizers, guides and other riders. If you have doubts about anything, ask. If you have always wanted to know how to do something, ask. If you want to know about preparing for a 100-mile sportive, find out who has done them, and learn from their experiences. And remember, take time to relax and enjoy the trip. Get extra sleep, put your feet up during the afternoon, enjoy a massage, visit the town – it is a break from home and from work, as well as a week of training.

Post camp

When you arrive home, use the following week as a recovery week. Do easier rides at a moderate pace to allow your body to properly recuperate. Reflect on what you learnt, what areas you were weakest at, and how you can work to improve them during the coming months. A camp is just one building block that can help you become a better sportive rider: it should be great fun and it should be productive, but only if you approach it correctly will it be so. It should also leave you with great memories and something to look forward to for the following year once the winter starts approaching again.

Experience Says …

- Set a goal for every training ride, and be selfish to your own needs if riding with others
- Build up the length of training rides to replicate the event you are training for
- Kick-start your metabolism and your ability to burn fat by riding before eating on one or two days a week
- Do not feel guilty about taking rest days
- Keep your promise to family members with regard to training time; broken commitments will lead to trouble
- Map out your events for the season, and plan when you really need to peak for events
- Drink a protein recovery drink after every training session
- Get plenty of sleep as your body needs time to recover between sessions
- Taper your training in the week leading up to an event
- Don't become a slave to the training plan – adapt it if necessary
- Rehearse the event – train as specifically as possible
- If you have a cold above the neck, train lightly; if below, take some time off.

CHAPTER 4

AVOIDING INJURIES AND IMPROVING FLEXIBILITY

There are always risks associated with participation in sporting activities, and cycling, especially in large groups, is no exception. Following the advice and guidelines on technique in this book will certainly help reduce the risk of injury. Using the correct equipment, having the bike set up properly, using the correct techniques whilst on the bike, and following nutritional guidelines will all help in the process of reducing injury. The information contained in the next section will also help you enjoy more injury-free rides.

Common Injuries

The worst case scenario is head or spinal injury. There is fierce debate as to the effectiveness of wearing a helmet when cycling – all we will say on this topic is that we are vehement supporters of wearing helmets, and will let those who disagree with that viewpoint make their own decisions. Whatever your standpoint, even when a helmet is worn, damage can occur to the head in high impact collisions, and a helmet will certainly not protect other areas of the body. Sub-standard or poorly fitted helmets can contribute to a certain amount of injuries. Other injuries include fractures, contusions and sprains or strains. The areas of the body most commonly affected are the wrists, shoulders, ankles and lower legs.

The most common injuries to cyclists are bruises and abrasions to the skin from falls on rough road surfaces, although handlebars and saddles have been implicated in a wide range of abdominal and genital injuries. Neck and back pain are common in cyclists, and in fact several nerves can be damaged by endurance cycling events unless you prepare properly and ride a correctly fitted bike.

These conditions arise primarily as a result of the bike having the wrong mechanics and inappropriate equipment, causing numbness in the fingers, genitalia and backside. Over-use injuries are very common and often come from a simple oversight such as incorrect riding position or cycling with too much pedal resistance. Recent research seems to show that over-use injuries are lower using lower gear ratios at a higher cadence – hence the importance of heeding advice on bike fit, gearing and pedalling technique.

Certain traumatic incidents cannot be avoided. Thankfully, anticipating any errors from other riders will minimize the risk of injury and make your cycling experiences all the more rewarding and enjoyable.

Improving Flexibility

For many years in sports it has been a commonly held belief that stretching before participating in an event can help the performance of the athlete and guard against injuries. More recent research may suggest otherwise, which will of course be sweet music to the ears of most cyclists who ride and get off without giving a thought to stretching. There is evidence, however, that static stretching can reduce some forms of injury as well as the incidence of muscle strains.

The Muscles Involved in Cycling

Stretching may or may not be as beneficial as we first thought, but there is still a place for it in the warm-up routine. We are believers in the usefulness of stretching as part of an overall preparation programme, and we firmly believe that stretching after cycling is beneficial. To perform appropriate stretches it is of course important to know what muscles are engaged in cycling, and which benefit from stretching.

Most people can name at least one or two muscles that are necessary to the action of cycling (probably from the leg), but there are several other muscles that are equally important to successfully propel you down the road. The muscles commonly associated with cycling are the quadriceps, gluteus and calf. These are extensor muscles that are responsible for the down-stroke phase of pedal motion. The flexor muscles, psoas, hamstrings, tibialis anterior and the extensor hallucis longus are also very important.

A strong core is also very important for a cyclist because it makes cycling more efficient, especially in the ranges required to be an endurance cyclist. This adds the abdominal muscles and the erector spinae group to the list of

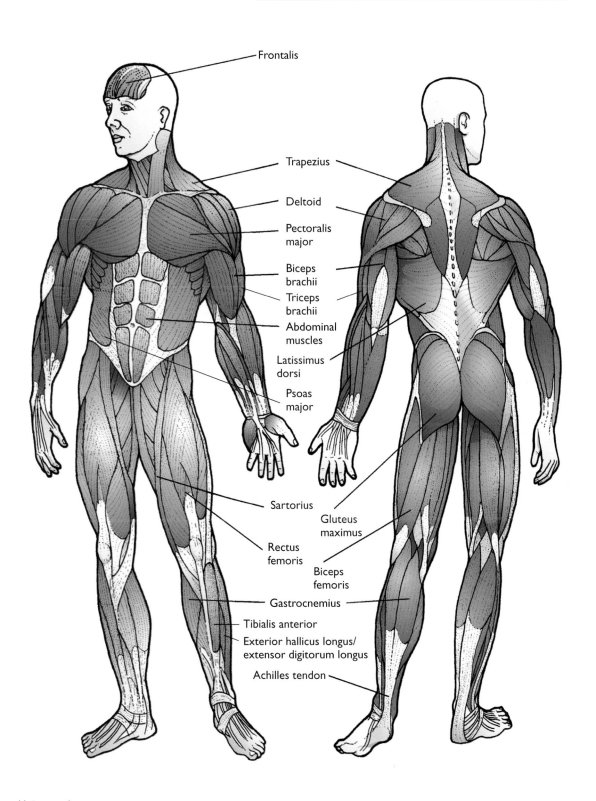

Frontalis

Trapezius

Deltoid

Pectoralis
major

Biceps
brachii

Triceps
brachii

Abdominal
muscles

Latissimus
dorsi

Psoas
major

Sartorius

Gluteus
maximus

Rectus
femoris

Biceps
femoris

Gastrocnemius

Tibialis anterior

Exterior hallicus longus/
extensor digitorum longus

Achilles tendon

Major muscle groups.

important muscles. Other muscles important to the cyclist are the triceps and extensors of the forearm.

Warm-Up Dynamic Stretches

Even though research suggests that stretching does not reduce the risk of injury nor enhance performance because of its other benefits it may still be incorporated into a warm-up routine. A standard warm-up before a training ride or sportive might consist of at least the dynamic stretches detailed below, then 5min on the bike at a relaxed pace.

The following stretches should be part of the pre-event routine and can form part of your overall preparation:

The Calf
Starting from a push-up position, push one heel towards the ground, then transfer the weight to the ball of that foot. Hold for a few seconds. Repeat ten times. Repeat using the opposite leg.

ABOVE AND BELOW: *Quadriceps and calf stretch.*

Calf stretch.

The Quadriceps and Calf
Keeping your back straight, place your feet shoulders width apart. Place one foot forwards, keeping your knee in line with the foot. Bend the trailing leg. Repeat five times with each leg.

The Iliotibial Band and Adductors

Holding on to the bike frame, swing one leg away from the body. Point the toes away from the body. Swing the leg back, then across the body, keeping the lower back fixed. Repeat ten times, then change legs.

The Hamstrings, Quadriceps, Psoas and Calf

Holding on to the bike frame, swing the outside leg forwards then backwards. Keep the lower back fixed. Repeat ten times, then change legs.

Iliotibial band and adductors.

Hamstrings, quadriceps, psoas and calf.

Neck stretch.

The Neck

Gently roll the head in a clockwise direction ten times. Change to an anticlockwise direction, and repeat.

Roadside Stretches

In sportive events, especially as a beginner, you may find that certain muscles or muscle groups tighten up as the event unfolds. When this happens it is a good idea to pause when at feed stations to perform a few simple stretches. Here are some examples.

The Back and Hamstrings

Lean against the bike with one hand on the saddle, the other on the handlebars. Arch your back pushing your pelvis towards the bike, and look up slightly; breathe in as you are doing this. As you breathe out, push your backside away from the bike and tilt forwards. Arch your spine backwards. Do this ten times.

Back and hamstring stretch.

Quadriceps.

The Quadriceps

Using the bike as support, stand next to it holding on to the seat. Reach back with your free arm and grab your ankle. Pull it towards your buttock, keeping the knees as close together as possible. Hold for a few seconds, then relax. Repeat ten times. Do the same with the opposite leg.

The Hamstrings

Support yourself by holding on to the handlebars. Place the heel of one foot on to the apex of the frame. Straighten your back leg and tilt your body towards the raised leg. Hold for a few seconds, then relax. Repeat ten times. Do the same with the opposite leg.

Hamstring.

Calf.

The Calf

Using your bike for support, place one leg behind you. Straighten your back leg as you lean towards the bike, being sure to keep your foot on the floor. Hold for a few seconds, then relax. Repeat ten times. Do the same with the opposite leg.

The Trapezius

Using the bike as an anchor, stand next to the frame, holding it with one hand. Making sure your shoulders are as level as possible, lift your free arm over your head. Place your hand on the side of your head nearest the bike. Gently pull your neck away from the bike. Hold for a few seconds, then relax. Repeat ten times. Do the same with the opposite shoulder.

Trapezius.

Stretching in the Saddle

If you are a more experienced rider you might want to stretch while you are riding. This requires a certain degree of skill and balance, be careful and aware of other riders around you. When stretching while on the move it is important to choose the right terrain. Make sure the part of the course you are on is essentially flat and that you are aware of the position of fellow riders. Increase your speed for a period so that you can comfortably freewheel while stretching.

The Quadriceps

Unclip one foot from the pedal. Grab the free ankle, and pull it backwards and upwards towards the saddle. Hold for a few seconds, then relax. Repeat. Do the same exercise with the other leg.

The Calf

Drop one heel towards the ground. Straighten that leg and lean forwards slightly. Hold for a few seconds, then relax. Repeat ten times. Do the same exercise with the other leg.

The Hamstring

Push your backside to the rear of the bike. Making sure the leg to be stretched is not quite straight, lean your body down (bending at the waist) and slightly forwards. Hold for a few seconds, then relax. Repeat. Do the same exercise with the other leg.

Back Muscles

Arch your back pushing your pelvis towards the front of the bike and look up slightly; breathe in as you are doing this. As you breathe out, push your backside towards the back of the bike, and tilt forwards. Arch your spine backwards. Repeat.

TOP: *On the bike: quadriceps.*
MIDDLE: *On the bike: calf.*
BOTTOM RIGHT: *On the bike: back stretch.*
BELOW: *On the bike: hamstring.*

Post-Ride Stretching

Stretching should also be part of your warm-down procedure – though again, there is debate as to the effectiveness
of stretches after an event. Nevertheless, after completing a
sportive, gentle stretching and massage is normally a wel-
comed experience. For the warm-up stretches we still
incorporate dynamic stretching; for the warm-down we
concentrate on static stretches.

The Quadriceps
Use a wall for support. Keep your back straight and pull
your heel towards your buttock. Try to keep the knees
as close together as possible. Hold for twenty seconds,
then relax. Do the same with the opposite leg.

The Calf
Use a wall for support. Place one leg behind the other.
Keeping the rear leg straight and the foot on the floor, bend
the front leg. Hold for twenty seconds, then relax. Do the
same with the opposite leg.

The Hamstring
Place one heel on a raised surface. Bend the other knee and
flex forwards at the hips. Hold for twenty seconds, then
relax. Do the same with the opposite leg.

The Lower Back
Lying on your back, bend the hips and knees 90 degrees.
Keeping your legs together, bring them to one side so they
are resting on the ground. Repeat, bringing the knees to the
opposite side of the body. Perform ten times each side.

Post ride: quadriceps.

Post ride: calf.

RIGHT: Post ride: lower back.

BELOW: Post ride: hamstring.

Other Stretches

These stretches can either be added to the above, or done separately.

Iliotibial Band

Start by kneeling on the floor. Place the hands on the floor with straight arms. Move one leg back so it is straight out behind your body. Move the other leg so that the lower part of the leg is in line with the straight leg. Tilt your body towards the side of the bent leg. Hold for twenty seconds, then relax. Do the same on the other side.

BELOW: Iliotibial band stretch.

Gluteal Muscles

Sit on a chair. Rest one ankle on the opposite knee. Link the fingers together and grab the flexed knee. Gently bring that knee towards the opposite shoulder. Hold for twenty seconds, then relax. Do the same with the opposite leg.

Gluteal muscle stretch.

Piriformis Muscle

Lie on your back. Bring your feet up so they are flat on the ground (knees bent). Place one ankle on the other knee. Bring one hand through both legs and the other to the outside of a leg. Clasp the hands together. Bring your hands closer to your torso. Hold for twenty seconds, then relax. Do the same with the opposite leg.

Piriformis muscle stretch.

THE OLDER ATHLETE

If you are joining the sport late, do not be put off by the fact that other competitors may be slightly younger than you, because in many ways you have a slight advantage when competing in endurance events. Put another way, everyone has two types of muscle fibres: fast twitch (type 2) fibres, and slow twitch (type 1) fibres. Fast twitch fibres are responsible for explosive movements such as sprinting, whereas slow twitch fibres are the fibres that help with endurance events. As you get older you lose a lot of your type 2 fibres, so relatively speaking you have more type 1 fibres. It is possible to maintain these by regular training. Interestingly, studies have shown that cyclists show less regression in performance with age than swimmers and runners.

There are, of course, changes that occur as we age, and it is useful to understand what happens, and to remember that activity and exercise can significantly slow down and reduce the impact of many of these natural ageing processes. The principal changes are:

- Bodyweight and body fat can increase
- Height decreases (from about forty years of age)
- Fat-free body mass decreases (from around forty-five years of age)
- Maximal muscle strength decreases
- Total number of muscle fibres decreases
- Maximal heart rate slows down and peak blood flow reduces, resulting in decreased oxygen transport to the muscles
- Flexibility declines

A balanced and specifically constructed stretching and training programme can counteract many of the effects of ageing, and many veteran sportive riders are still turning in impressive finishing times in the toughest events.

CHAPTER 5

NUTRITION: CONSUME TO PERFORM

Be aware that no two sportive riders are identical, and no two training plans or dietary regimes will be the same. Life also has a habit of getting in the way of strict regimes, be they training plans or eating plans, so be prepared to adapt and modify to suit family, work, travel or other circumstances. The secret lies in maintaining an overall balance of consumption and establishing a predictable, balanced intake of the correct nutritional elements in more or less the correct quantities, most of the time. This is good news for those with less than iron wills, because it means you can indulge every now and then and still reach your goals.

Fuel or Food?

For committed sportive riders it can be helpful to think of food and drink not as pleasures, but as sources of fuel that support other training activities and help us stay fit, healthy, and ready to complete the challenge ahead. Think about intake as a straight mathematical calculation: take in less than you need and you will lose fitness, health and the ability to perform at your best; take in more than you need and you are likely to gain body fat and deliver a substandard result.

Aim to maintain a diet that supplies your training and living needs and leaves you with a small amount of energy in reserve; an endurance athlete's diet is a long-term event, just like the event itself. The overall objective is to reach your optimum power-to-weight ratio – this is cycling's ultimate goal.

Also be aware that each individual has a different physique and 'engine', and the variations between these can be huge. So don't try to be someone else, but plan your nutritional strategy specifically for your own metabolism, physiology and objectives.

You Are What You Eat

What you eat and drink will have a direct impact on your energy levels and ability to perform. In general terms, an endurance cyclist's diet will reduce the proportion of saturated fats such as fried foods and dairy products (other than milk, perhaps), and will increase the proportion of carbohydrates such as pasta, potatoes, bananas and rice. The average sportive rider carbo-loading for an event may well need to take in around 7g of carbohydrate for every kilogram of bodyweight in the two or three days leading up to the event, and if possible the bulk of this should be derived from unrefined carbohydrates such as brown rice or wholewheat pasta. On the day of the event itself, switch the carbohydrate intake to refined carbohydrates with a high glycaemic index that can be absorbed quickly by the body; these might include cereals, rice, potatoes, honey and fruit juices.

Eat Natural

But that's only part of the story, because your body needs protein such as fish and meat to rebuild tissue and increase muscle, and also essential vitamins and minerals, often found in vegetables. The way you cook food also contributes to the value and benefit you gain from it, so try to remove fat from meat, eat white rather than red meat, and don't overcook vegetables and other foods thereby removing their maximum nutritional benefit. Avoid eating processed or 'fast'

A WORD OF CAUTION

Many committed cyclists become obsessed with weight loss and body fat percentages. Maintaining a healthy level of body fat and overall weight is central to maintaining a healthy immune system: drop too far, and you will be at greater risk of infection, illness and general fatigue. Our recommendation is to establish where you are at the outset, set a realistic and sensible goal (maybe taking expert advice), and then work steadily and progressively towards a goal over a period of time, changing diet and nutritional practices progressively. The outcome will be more sustainable and more likely to remain in place than will be delivered by a sudden change and a drastic regime.

Finally, don't forget that in addition to your training and competing needs (a 100-mile event might use 5,000 calories or thereabouts) you also need to fuel daily life and your base metabolism; for an average adult male that means about 2,500 calories a day, and for a woman around 1,900. So on a training day, if you burn 1,500 calories through exercise, you will need to take in around 3,500 to 4,000 calories just to remain level. Take in a few less and gradually you will shed body fat. But be careful – there's no value in being the skinniest but most unhealthy and slowest cyclist in the sportive. And in our experience there are plenty of thin, gaunt-looking cyclists who never seem well enough to do that training ride or complete that event.

Carry two 500ml or even 750ml bottles in an event.

foods, high saturated fat foods and high refined sugar foods. Also try to make sure you consume a good intake of fatty acids such as omega 3, so include oily fish such as mackerel or salmon in your diet.

During an Event

During an event you may well utilize energy bars, gels and carbohydrate drinks to deliver essential fuel, but another tip is not to use these valuable supplements for the first time during an event, but to make sure you establish what suits you, and what your body assimilates easily and comfortably, well in advance of race day. There has now been enough research to show that the intake of energy drinks with the right balance of carbohydrate, protein and other essential minerals can increase endurance and deliver energy more efficiently to the body than water alone.

Fluid Intake

Fluid intake is a critical part of fuelling and nutrition. While training for an event you should aim to increase fluid intake; there is no better fluid than water for general consumption, but juices and other drinks will suit some people. It is clear, however, that carefully balanced energy drinks can boost performance and extend endurance; a typical drink might include four parts carbohydrate to one part protein. During an event, therefore, aim to take on board up to 1ltr of water an hour, to replace around the same number – that is, 1kg of weight loss. Fluid consumption does vary from rider

to rider, so it is important to establish your own requirements before testing it in an event.

During training and in routine daily life try to drink at the very least a couple of litres a day, and more when training hard or for long periods. Fluid consumption is one area where there are dramatic differences between individuals, but few people will go wrong if they consume a fairly substantial quantity of pure, fresh water every day, supplemented by specifically formulated energy drinks during an event. Remember, 5 per cent dehydration results in as much as 20 per cent performance decrease – so keep drinking.

A Balanced Hydration Plan

The following plan is an example of how and what to drink during an ordinary, non-event day. It is a guideline or framework, because basically there is no limit to how much you can and should drink (within reason); however, a varied intake containing different drinks will add to your enjoyment and make sure you develop the fluid intake habit.

07:00hr: Wake-up cup of green tea or red-bush tea: full of antioxidants but also containing catechins, which assist in the utilization of fat during exercise. Recent research has also shown that green tea may help to boost performance during endurance exercise. For people with sensitivity to caffeine, red-bush tea is naturally caffeine free.

09:00hr: Glass of orange juice: it replaces lost minerals including potassium, but also contains other essential elements including electrolytes and vitamin C.

11:00hr: Glass of water: too many benefits to name, but a critical part of the nutritional and training regime.

13:00hr: Glass of cherry juice dilute: crammed with antioxidants, but also a natural anti-inflammatory and pain relief agent. Research has shown that cherry juice (from the dark-skinned varieties) can assist in reducing muscle pain during endurance events.

15:00hr: Cup of coffee: a quick caffeine boost to help you through the rest of the day, or prepare you for a training session after work; coffee also contains niacin, which is essential in the production of red blood cells.

17:00hr: Just before the after-work training ride, use a sports energy drink to fuel yourself for the session. A balanced sports drink will contain various electrolytes, carbohydrates and other essential elements.

19:00hr: After the training session, use a protein recovery drink made with skimmed milk, or simply milk itself within the first half an hour after exercise to replace lost muscle glycogens and deliver protein for tissue recovery.

22:00hr: End the evening with a cup of milk or chocolate drink; it contains an amino acid called tryptophan which increases serotonin levels in the body, promoting relaxation.

But remember: fresh, clean water is the key ingredient in your everyday intake, so use the other drinks for specific reasons and sip water all through the day at regular intervals. We would normally carry a water bottle around wherever we go, making sure that we maintain hydration at all times. It may feel strange at first to wander around with a water bottle in your hand, but after a while it becomes second nature.

The Benefits of a Healthy Diet

Diet directly affects performance, in both the short and the long term. A good diet will support and underpin repeated training efforts such as are required during the build-up to a sportive. There is no single regime that suits every athlete, and every individual's needs will change and evolve over time and in relation to their programme. Fuel and fluid replacement are critical elements of the overall training plan, and need to become embedded components in the lifestyle of the sportive rider.

To summarize the benefits of a good nutritional regime: it will ensure optimal gains from both training and recovery periods, the development of the desired physique and physical attributes, reduced risk of injury and ill-health, and even greater enjoyment and motivation from the exercise programme.

Weight Loss, Recovery and Health

As mentioned above, an individual should plan a nutrition regime to suit their own goals and needs, and not try to replicate another athlete's programme. Moreover, when managing a nutritional strategy, the individual should eat/fuel to meet their needs, and not always in response to appetite or hunger. Thus a balanced intake of carbohydrate, protein, vitamins and minerals should be delivered on a regular basis: it is quite usual for someone in serious training to eat as many as five or even six times a day, because small and often is better than large and seldom. What is important, of course, is that the intake is made up of the right elements, so no snacking on chocolate bars and chips – or at least, very little snacking.

It is also very helpful to establish a start point and to monitor progress and results on a regular basis; keeping a simple record of weight or body fat will both maintain focus and motivate as goals are reached. A warning here, however: it is quite common for an individual to notice a slight weight increase at the start of a long-term training programme, because muscle bulk (dense and heavy) increases faster than body fat disappears. Don't panic: keep the regime going, and the body fat will begin to drop away.

Losing Weight

To facilitate weight loss and body fat reduction, start to make a switch to lower fat or unsaturated fat foodstuffs – from full fat to skimmed milk, for example, or from butter to olive oil spread. To support training and recovery, achieve a balance between fat, carbohydrate and protein requirements. In very broad terms, calorie consumption should be split 25 per cent fat, 35 per cent protein and 40 per cent carbohydrate. Different metabolisms and training programmes will require variations on these proportions, and different types of training effort and intensity will require that the proportions will have to be adjusted. For example, after intensive power intervals the level of protein intake will be increased to help the body repair and rebuild damaged or stressed muscle tissue.

The average individual training regularly for an endurance event may need at least 1.5g of protein per kilo of bodyweight per day – but even at this elevated level of requirement, you can get all you need from a normal, healthy, balanced diet. After a hard training session, however, the body's glycogen stores are depleted and the muscles are torn and inflamed. Toxins have built up, which need to be removed and attacked by natural defence and repair mechanisms. So the refuelling process requires the intake of carbohydrates, protein, fluid and salts. Carbohydrates replenish muscle glycogen reserves, and protein is a vital factor in muscle regeneration. The consumption of beneficial fats is also necessary for the sportive rider, since 1g of fat supplies

GOOD FOODS/BASIC ELEMENTS

Carbohydrate	Proteins	Fats	Vegetables and fruits
Cereals	White fish	Monounsaturated fats	Broccoli
Porridge	Chicken	Polyunsaturated fats	Spinach
Rice	Red meat	Olive oil	Salads
Breads	Eggs	Peanuts/cashews	Tomatoes and fresh fruits
Potatoes	Milk		
Pasta	Cheese		
Bananas			
Figs			
Honey			

around nine calories of energy – more than twice the calories available from either carbohydrates or protein.

Very recent research seems to indicate that high fibre, protein-rich foods consumed in conjunction with carbohydrates have the effect of reducing hunger, which can help in a gradual weight loss programme. There is also evidence that this combination optimizes muscle and general recovery. But whatever the combination you choose, above all else it is essential to eat well and to match calorie intake to calorie expenditure.

Recovery

A golden rule of nutritional intake is: always try to refuel with an hour – and better still, within half an hour – of the exercise, as the body's ability to replace energy stores is at its best in that window. Research has shown that a higher rate of glycogen storage takes place in the two hours following exercise, and the ideal window for this is within twenty minutes.

An ideal recovery meal is a mixture of carbohydrate and protein – a little over 1g of carbohydrate per kilogram of bodyweight, with around 15g of protein; or put another way, eat a couple of large slices of bread and drink ½ltr of milkshake. After a sportive event we would always take on board a protein/carbohydrate replacement drink, although recent research suggests that plain, good old milk is as effective. A smoothie with skimmed milk, an apple and a banana, or a bowl of cereal with a slice of toast and peanut

butter, would do the job equally well. Whatever your personal choice – banana, carrot cake, milk or high-tech drink – try to consume it as soon as possible after the event, or after a long training session.

To summarize some ingredients of a good cycling diet, the above table includes foods that really should form a substantial part of your diet, whether as part of a meal or as a stand-alone item.

Health and Wellbeing

The process of training and competing stresses the body and causes a breakdown in muscle tissue and fibre as well as a depletion in essential minerals and salts. The period immediately after intense exercise is one of the most vulnerable times for an athlete, as the immune system is at its lowest.

It is essential to try to replace lost elements in order to be able to perform repeated efforts as required by the process of training for a sportive event.

Minerals such as copper, magnesium, iron, sodium, zinc and others are lost through sweat and the processes occurring as the body functions under the stress of exercise. Calcium is essential for the maintenance of strong and healthy bones, and antioxidants perform a vital role in the 'clean-up' operation required to deal with toxins and waste materials generated by the burning of fuel and oxygen by the muscles.

In order to maintain a healthy immune system and replace lost elements, a training diet should include a substantial proportion of fruit and vegetables as well as being balanced in terms of carbohydrate, fat and protein. Several portions of fruit and vegetables a day will provide everything required, but supplementation is often used as another simple way to ensure sufficient intake.

When you exercise, your body goes through a process of oxidative stress. Harmful molecules – known as 'free radicals' – increase in number and consume greater amounts of oxygen, with multiple effects: in the short term they cause increased stiff or sore muscles, muscle fatigue, and exposure to infection and illness; in the long term there can be more

---

ALCOHOL

As regards alcohol, the good news is that the body prefers to achieve and maintain a sensible balance, not necessarily total abstinence. So a moderate intake of alcohol does no harm, and many studies have suggested it may actually promote wellbeing. Red wine, for example, is rich in antioxidants and is generally regarded as helpful in smallish quantities. You might, having said all that, benefit from a period of restraint before the premier event in your schedule for the season, but we wouldn't want to dictate.

serious consequences. An increased intake of antioxidants from fruit and vegetables in particular combats these harmful effects and protects your long-term wellbeing.

A simple guideline when managing a diet is to select colourful fruits and vegetables for every meal; there is an interesting link between brightly coloured fruit and vegetable and a high concentration of antioxidant and vitamins. So match your meal to your training outfit and go for colour … and make sure you eat your greens …

Again, there are certain foods that we would always include as part of our routine diet, and the following are beneficial antioxidants and vitamin-bearing foods:

- Broccoli
- Carrot
- Cherries
- Tomato
- Berries
- Kiwi fruit
- Green vegetables
- Oily fish (mackerel, salmon, sardines)
- Citrus fruits.

Wonder Foods

There are some foods that are so beneficial that they should form part of any would-be athlete's diet; they deliver either multiple essential ingredients, or are high in a specific nutrient. These few items are at the heart of our own dietary regime – meaning that we would consume at least several portions of these every week, even if not every day. They include the following:

Porridge/oats: Contain slow-release carbohydrates perfect for endurance activity, and which are low in saturated fats, high in fibre and rich in beta glucan, which lowers cholesterol and boosts the immune system. Oats contain numerous phytochemicals that are powerful antioxidants, preventing cell damage. We recommend starting the day with a bowl of porridge made with skimmed milk, and doubling that on the morning of a sportive.

Apples: Contain multiple vitamins and also quercetin, which supports the immune system. We recommend munching your way through at least an apple a day, as the doctor said.

Bananas: Containing zero fat and one of the fastest and most easily digested sources of carbohydrate, bananas are also high in potassium and other essential elements. We would normally eat two a day before and during an event or training. Potassium intake also helps avoid cramping during an event.

Oily fish: Rich in omega 3, 6 and 9 fats, which are essential for the body to function properly. We would have several meals a week that include fish such as mackerel and salmon – they are also a source of protein and other elements of the basic diet.

Milk: Replenishes energy stores as fast as a recovery drink, with a natural blend of carbohydrates and protein. Recent research shows that milk also rehydrates the body as fast as, or faster than, other fluids. We use skimmed milk, and once the initial switch from full fat or semi-skimmed has been made, you never notice the difference.

Tart cherries (such as Morello, Montmorency): Extremely high in antioxidants, and now shown to actively reduce inflammation during exercise. We use diluted cherry drink as a training fluid, and carry a weak solution around in our water bottles most days.

Dark chocolate: Minimum 80 per cent cocoa: contains cocoa flavanols, a specific subset of flavanoids, which are powerful antioxidants, and have been shown to have a beneficial effect on sports performance. Researchers in Australia have demonstrated that a cocoa drink may help lower blood pressure, boost blood flow to the muscles, and reduce the demand placed on the heart during exercise. Cocoa also contains a whole host of other beneficial elements including vitamins, calcium and mag-nesium, a powerful antioxidant, and caffeine, which has long been associated with increased performance. A couple of squares of dark chocolate every day can both help the overall nutritional intake, and act as the 'treat of the day'.

Sample Diets

We are not going to dictate what you should and shouldn't eat any more than we have to; it's too easy to try to impose rules and regimes, but as we said in the training section and others, life has a habit of getting in the way of carefully laid or excessively rigid plans. So opposite are two examples of our own nutritional profile – our preferred/ideal, when we are maybe based at home, or at the weekend, or in a situation to be able to pick and choose – and then also the 'compromise' intake when work, travel or family disrupt the regime.

We are not professional athletes and we are the same as you – fairly committed, focused and keen individuals willing to make some sacrifices and to compromise in order to achieve our objective, without being Trappist monks or slaves to any single plan. We do stray from the path occasionally, and chocolate bars, extra glasses of wine, portions of fries and other assorted taboo items do find their way into our digestive systems from time to time … or should we say, if we're honest, at regular intervals …

Nevertheless, the message is simple: for the vast majority of us, as long as the indulgences are in the minority of the intake, and as long as an overall balance is maintained, then if the training hours are done and the lifestyle is healthy and balanced, the results will follow.

We have also included some examples of diets which illustrate how you can take on board the right fuels in the right quantities for both normal daily life and then for pre-event carbohydrate loading. These are ideas only, however, and you should feel free to adapt and modify your diet according to what is available and where you find yourself.

Example 1: Suggested Daily Diet

The following is a view of a preferred daily intake on a day where we can choose the time and ingredients of our nutritional intake. This is genuinely an accurate reflection of at least a couple of days a week in our schedule during a training period:

Pre-ride (06:30hr): One slice of wholewheat bread with manuka honey, or banana, with a cup of red-bush tea.

Ride (07:00 to 09:30hr): No intake, once or twice a week. Other days, one gel sachet, 0.5 to 1ltr cherry concentrate/water.

Post-ride (09:30hr/10:00hr): Medium bowl of large flake, rolled oats/porridge made with skimmed milk, a dessertspoon of manuka honey, a large glass protein/carbohydrate recovery drink made with skimmed milk, plus one scoop of whey protein, and a large glass of orange juice diluted with water.

'Elevenses' (mid/late morning): Omelette with two free-range eggs and mushrooms, made with olive oil and skimmed milk. A slice of wholewheat bread with olive oil spread. A cup of red-bush tea. A large glass of water.

Lunch (13:30/14:00hr): Tuna or peanut butter sandwich on wholewheat bread. A large glass of water.

Mid-afternoon (15:30/16:00hr): A cup of red-bush tea or hot chocolate with skimmed milk. Currant bun or scone, or sliced banana/carrot cake. A piece of fruit.

Dinner (19:15/19:30hr): Skinless chicken or duck breast, or pork or lean meat, or white fish, or pie with pastry in winter. One or two vegetables from spinach, broccoli, cabbage, green beans, kale or salad. Baked or boiled potato or rice or pasta. Large glass of water. A glass of red wine.

Through the evening: Glass of red wine, two squares of dark (80 per cent cocoa) chocolate.

Pre-sleep (2200hrs): A cup of hot skimmed milk.
That all sounds a lot as it is written down, but consider the calories used during the day – typically 1,500 to 1,750 during the 2½ hour ride, and then another 2,000 to 2,500 to

support the metabolism – therefore an intake of 3,500 to 4,250 simply to maintain equilibrium. It may be worth mentioning here that BJ is a shade under 6ft tall, weighs 77kg, and maintains a body fat level of around 9 per cent all year round.

Example 2: Compromise Daily Diet

When business or other commitments get in the way of things, then it is time to adapt and compromise, and there is no point getting annoyed with oneself about this. Try to stay somewhere along the guidelines of the 'Master Plan' but eat what's available and don't get too worried about having a day or two away from the ideal profile:

Breakfast (07:00hr): Bowl of porridge with manuka honey, or cereal with a banana. Large glass of orange juice diluted with water.

In-car or while travelling (07:30–09:30hr): Pre-meetings: 0.5ltr cherry juice diluted with water. Peanut butter or honey wholewheat sandwich or plain croissant, freshly squeezed orange juice and an apple.

Mid-morning (11:00hr): Cup of green or red-bush tea.

Lunch (13:30hr): Caesar salad or tuna sandwich, or if having a full lunch out, then white meat or chicken or fish with potato or rice or pasta and two green vegetables. Glass of white wine plus a large glass of water.

Late afternoon/return journey (17:00/18:00hr): Pack of cashew nuts or energy bar, a bottle of water.

Dinner (19:30/20:00hr): If you had a full lunch, then cheese and biscuits, or just a sandwich only. If you had a light lunch, then as per the preferred day above.

Evening: A glass of red wine and two squares of dark (80 per cent cocoa) chocolate.

Pre-sleep (22:00hr): A cup of hot skimmed milk.

Example 3: Carbohydrate Loading Plan for a 75–80kg Rider

The following is an example of a way to carbo-load before an event; it is appropriate for a male rider of around 75kg in weight. The loading should be started two to three days before the event itself:

Breakfast/early morning (07:00hr): Two cups of cereal with skimmed milk, plus 250ml of orange juice, one banana, and two slices of wholewheat toast with honey. Total 150g.

Mid-morning (11:00hr): 500ml of fruit juice or soft drink. Total 50g.

Midday/lunchtime (12:00/13:00hr): One bread roll with olive spread and peanut butter, plus one teacake, muffin or similar with jam, and one fruit smoothie drink. Total 150g.

Mid-afternoon (15:00hr): One fruit-flavoured yoghurt plus 250ml fruit juice. Total 50g.

Dinner (19:00hr): Three cups of pasta with sauce, plus two cups of mixed fruit salad, two scoops of ice cream, and a 500ml sports drink. Total 200g.

Late evening (22:00hr): Two squares dark chocolate. Total 50g.

Alongside these carbohydrates, you would add in other items including protein from meat (perhaps the pasta sauce) and fat (perhaps using olive spread and olive oil for cooking).

Example 4: Carbohydrate Loading Plan for a 60–67kg Rider

This plan is based on the requirements of a 60kg individual:

Breakfast (07:00hr): One large bowl of cereal or porridge with skimmed milk and raisins, plus one slice of toast with honey, and one glass of fruit juice.

Mid-morning (11:00hr): Banana sandwich.

Lunch (12:00 to 13:00hr): One baked potato with tinned tuna, plus salad and olive oil/vinegar dressing, two pieces of fruit and two pancakes.

Mid-afternoon (15:00hr): One banana plus a carton of yoghurt and a 250ml drink.

Dinner (19:00hr): A large bowl of pasta with chicken breasts with sauce, plus vegetables or a salad, followed by a bowl of fruit salad with low fat custard.

Late evening (22:00hr): A bowl of cereal and skimmed milk, plus one banana.

Example 5: Pre-Event Meal

Each of the following combinations provides around 150g of carbohydrate, to be mixed into a pre-event meal to set you up for the sportive:

- Two or three cups of breakfast cereal or oats, plus a banana plus skimmed milk

- Bread roll or three slices of toast with olive oil spread and honey
- Two cups of plain boiled rice plus two slices of bread or toast
- Four pancakes with syrup
- One energy bar with a fruit smoothie.

Again, other foods to provide a small intake of protein and fat may be used alongside these, but the focus should be on carbohydrate.

The Real World

We aren't claiming that these diets are perfect or that they conform to a nutritionist's ideal plan, but we live in the real world and we enjoy a wide range of food. Crisps, fries, chocolate bars and wine all creep in to our consumption, but in moderation and alongside a fairly high mileage training schedule. Overall we feel that the ingredients are generally the right type of items, and the balance is more or less right. We rarely drink beer these days, we use skimmed milk rather than full fat, and we usually use olive oil or vegetable spreads rather than butter. Milk chocolate very, very occasionally passes our lips, although in general we stay away from excessively sweet and sugary things.

By keeping our diets in context with both our working and training lives, we have gradually and consistently reached weight and health levels that seem to work for us. We recommend that you develop your own regimes and patterns for yourself, and once again, don't try to be someone else or adopt a regime that is simply impractical for your lifestyle.

Experience Says …

- Eat a balanced diet – approximately 50 per cent carbohydrate, 30 per cent protein, 20 per cent fat
- Lose weight slowly and progressively – don't use crash diets, and don't reduce body fat to dangerous levels
- Incorporate 'superfoods' into your diet – cocoa, oatmeal, berries, cherries, bananas
- Drink frequently – stay hydrated
- Don't skip breakfast – it sets you up for the day and triggers the right metabolic processes
- Prefer white meats and fish to red meats, avoid saturated fats
- Minimize the use of processed foods, and use fresh foods when they are in season
- Include fruit, salad and vegetables at every meal
- Replenish your body fuel stores within 30 minutes of exercise – this is the optimal recovery/replenishment window.

CHAPTER 6

TECHNIQUE

So you have the bike, you've got the kit, you're eating the right things, you look the part and you are ready to ride. Yet as Steve Hegg, Olympic gold medallist, says: 'Bikes don't win races, riders do.' The interaction between bike, equipment, the rider and other road users needs to be balanced, and any one element will affect the performance of the others. This chapter therefore sets out to help you learn and improve the skills required to ride safely, with confidence, at speed and in a group.

A Word on Safety

Before we talk about the correct technique to use when riding your bike, it is important to cover some fundamentals of riding safely, be it in an event or on a training ride. Most of the time your safety is in your own hands, but especially when riding in traffic or in a group (and sometimes both) you are often at the mercy of other road users. The following advice will help you ride safely.

Ride Predictably

- Above all else, ride in a confident and assertive manner, because riding that way will give other road users the confidence that they know what you are doing. Clearly signal your intent and execute manoeuvres positively and decisively
- Indicate clearly when turning – hold your arm out parallel to the ground to signal the direction of your turn. Look over your shoulder before you signal, check the traffic conditions, and signal well in advance of the manoeuvre. Pull out well in advance of the turn and hold your position.

Expect Cars To Be Unpredictable

- Be especially careful of cars overtaking you and then immediately turning left across you. Drivers will often pull out of junctions without seeing you, or will turn across you. It is your responsibility to anticipate these actions and protect yourself
- When riding past a line of parked cars make sure you provide enough room so that if someone did open a door you would not be knocked off. If there are spaces between the cars do not weave in and out
- As you ride behind cars get used to looking through the rear window to spot any movement in the car or in front of it. This way you can anticipate a door opening, a pedestrian stepping out, or a car about to pull out
- When you stop for a traffic light, position yourself towards the centre of the lane to prevent drivers trapping you against the curb. It is very easy, especially ahead of a left turn, for drivers not to see you and to turn across you
- When traffic is queuing, ride in the centre of your lane – you will be as fast as the moving traffic and it stops drivers attempting to squeeze through, putting you at risk
- If you do get into an altercation with a motorist remember that generally there can only be one winner in a battle between a car and a bike. Back off, move on, or let the motorist get away.

Why is Good Technique So Important?

Some of the greatest bike riders through history have used fantastic technique to deliver efficiency and power beyond their rivals. Riders such as Fausto Coppi, Hugo Koblet, Jacques Anquetil, Lance Armstrong and more recently Fabian Cancellara or Andy Schleck honed their technique across all elements of bike riding to gain an advantage on their competitors. As a sportive rider, a good, smooth technique can save 10 per cent of energy over a 100-mile event, and is a key determinant of speed, safety and enjoyment.

The basis of good technique centres around your pedalling, gearing and minimizing drag through an effective aerodynamic position on the bike.

Pedalling

At a cadence of ninety revolutions per minute, a six-hour 100-mile event requires around 32,000 pedal strokes per leg, so you can appreciate the cumulative effects of incorrect or ineffective pedalling technique. The ability to turn your pedals smoothly, at a consistent pace, and in a way that does not overstress your muscles, is the foundation of good performance in a sportive. The riders of old coined an

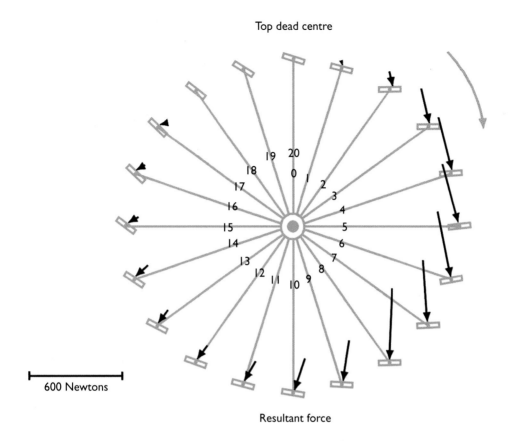

Top dead centre

Resultant force

600 Newtons

The anatomy of a pedal stroke.

expression to describe a smooth, fluid pedalling action: they called it '*la suplesse*'. Perhaps the greatest exponent was Hugo Koblet, the so-called 'pedaller of charm', who would often take out a comb as he rode a steep climb and run it through his hair while maintaining an apparently effortless, smooth pedalling action. This had the effect of demoralizing his opponents immediately. Koblet had a naturally smooth, circular and fluent riding style that was immensely efficient and economical.

So in an effort to replicate this smooth, effective style, let us look at the mechanics of the pedal stroke to understand what contributes to optimal technique.

Pedal Motion

The force you apply during a single pedal stroke changes through the complete revolution of the pedal action, as shown in the diagram above. When force is applied in the most effective way you produce torque, which is what propels the bike forward. Wasted effort through the pedal stroke means reduced torque, which in turn leads to tiredness and, in a sportive, underperformance. If you spend time improving your pedal motion your power and efficiency will be effectively increased.

The force applied starts from position zero (top, dead centre). The crank and pedal are shown in relation to each other through the stroke. How hard you pedal is shown by the length of the arrow, and the angle of the arrow shows the direction in which your force is being applied.

Most cyclists attain peak force at position four, but you also see significant downward force is still being applied at the bottom of the stroke (position ten). What may be a surprise is that there remains an element of downward force applied even through the upstroke (positions eleven through to fourteen), which is, in effect, slowing down the other leg during its corresponding downstroke. The ability to reduce this downward force in the latter phases of the pedal stroke is key to improving your torque and therefore the overall effectiveness of, and output from, your pedalling action.

The above of course applies equally to pedalling while sitting down or standing.

Leg position through the pedal stroke.

Improving Pedal Motion

One of the easiest ways to improve pedal motion is to practise single leg pedalling – that is, pedalling with one leg only, with the other away from the pedal and crank. This is most easily done on a static bike or turbo trainer, but is an exercise that can be introduced into a training ride in the open air quite easily.

Start by unclipping your right foot from the pedal. Pedal using the left leg for one minute, and note how you will 'feel' the force through the entire pedal revolution in a way that is very difficult to gauge when cycling with both feet. You will become more aware of the zone that propels the bike forwards (positions two to seven), and also the effect that you can achieve by relieving downward pressure through positions nine to sixteen. The ability to reduce downward force in the latter positions will increase the torque produced by your opposing leg, meaning that more of your power is effectively used to propel the bike forwards.

After one minute, change legs and repeat the exercise.

Gradually build up the time spent practising on each leg until you can comfortably ride for five minutes on each side. As you then take the technique on to the road you will notice that your legs will feel lighter in the upstroke, which will result in faster progress with less effort.

The Importance of Cadence

One common mistake we see in events is riders expending too much energy by pushing too high a gear – rocking from side to side in enormous efforts to turn the pedals at an incredibly slow pace. The pace at which you turn your pedals is called your cadence.

Essentially a rider with a slow cadence is putting more effort into pushing the pedals, resulting in a very slow pedal action (typically between sixty and eighty revolutions per minute). While this can produce high speed for short periods, it is rarely sustainable over the entirety of a sportive event as muscles fatigue.

Of course, a slow cadence could be because this naturally suits your style, but equally it could be because you have 'run out of gears' – typically caused by the top gear on your rear cassette being too high (a twenty-three or twenty-five tooth as opposed to a twenty-seven or twenty-nine), or you not having enough power in your legs! So a fast cadence saves energy, reduces fatigue, and better enables you to respond to changes in pace, all of which are vital in a sportive.

Riders will have a natural cadence, but an increase in your average can be a skill that is learned with practice. This can be achieved in two ways: by spinning sets, and by riding a fixed-gear bike.

Spinning Sets

Some cyclists are not inclined to do regimented drills, but you can still incorporate high cadence work into your rides to increase efficiency.

Find a flat stretch of road where you can ride uninterrupted for several minutes. Shift into a very easy gear, and time how long it takes to get to the end of the road without shifting. Repeat the exercise using different gears and note the change in time and also your perceived level of effort. This will help you feel the right balance between speed, force and tiredness.

Fixed-Gear Bikes

Another way to build leg strength and improve pedalling mechanics at the same time is to ride a fixed-gear bike – that is, a bike with a single gear on the rear. A fixed-gear has no freewheel, which means that whenever the bike is moving the pedals are moving too, as they are directly linked. Forget to pedal for a second on a fixed-gear bike, and the bike reminds you by thrusting your legs through the pedal stroke with or without your permission. The feeling can be jarring, and at high speed potentially dangerous, so be careful to build your speed and confidence over time. Since fixed-gear bikes have only one gear, the same gear is obviously used to get up a hill as to ride back down it, and that provides a strength session as well, as you grind the cranks up the slope without being able to change down into an easier gear.

Many fixed-gear bikes have a 'flip-flop' rear hub whereby you can remove the rear wheel, turn it round and use a gear on the other side that has a freewheel hub. The freewheel allows you to stop pedalling and to coast as you would on a geared bike. For 'real world' riding on the roads, a freewheel hub is probably a more practical solution than a fixed-gear.

With a single gear you will find climbing hills of any significance becomes a focused effort to maintain your cadence, and will often mean climbing out of the saddle to maintain momentum. This also gives your legs practice at pulling up on the 'recovery' (rear) quadrant of the pedal stroke. Once the road drops downwards again, the legs have to spin at a very high cadence to keep up with the rear wheel down the other side, providing very effective, even if inelegant, high-cadence practice.

Fixed-gear bikes are cheap, too. A new one can cost less than £300, or an old bike can be converted to a 'fixie' by removing the derailleur and cables, and buying a wheel with a fixed-gear hub. Check, however, that the frame has rear-facing dropouts (the slots into which the wheel axle slides), as this allows you to position the rear wheel to tension the chain.

With enough high-cadence spinning practice, a smoother pedal stroke becomes second nature. Routinely taking time out to work on your pedal action will enable you to better adjust your speeds and save energy through an optimal cadence. You won't get dropped when the terrain requires a quick gear change, you can spin up hills without your legs loading up with lactic acid, and you can save your muscles for when you really have to push on in an event.

Selecting the Right Gear

Selection of the correct gear at the right time is a very important element in maintaining an even pace and controlling energy expenditure through a sportive. Your ability to spare your legs to keep them fresh is a useful skill, and intelligent use of your gears is a great way to do this. It is therefore crucial to decide when to change gear, to anticipate shifts and to shift often, to avoid cross-chaining, to listen to more experienced riders, and not to coast down the other side of a steep climb.

When to Change Gear

It is important to scan the terrain ahead of you in order to plan the correct gear, or range of gears, that you will need. It is easy to focus on the road or the riders immediately in front of you, and arrive at a section of road for which you are in the wrong combination of front ring and rear gears.

Ideally, you should focus on keeping the chain in the middle of the rear cassette – this will give you the most options in terms of shifting up or down as the terrain requires. As the chain is the part of the bike that has the

This position gives you the greatest scope for changing gear.

Starting a climb in this combination of 'small to small' offers you flexibility.

most working parts, any drag or resistance should be minimized – so the straighter the chain's line, the less tension it will have.

As you get towards the inner or outer gears on the rear sprocket you should consider the position on the inner or outer ring on the front. If you are approaching the upper limit of your rear cassette and you are still on the large ring on the front, then you should consider changing the smaller ring on the front and then immediately shifting the chain to a smaller sprocket on the rear until you have matched the previous effort on the big ring.

If you get this right, then you can carry greater speed into corners and other road sections by rapidly changing up through the gears, or, and more importantly, you can avoid hitting a sharp climb with the chain on the large ring at the front and your largest sprocket on the rear cassette.

It is therefore important to appreciate the key to maintaining momentum through correct use of the gears.

Anticipate Shifts

It is very difficult (and bad for your bike) to change gears when you are pushing the pedals very hard. So get into the habit of downshifting into an easier gear as you begin to approach a climb; this will make it easier on your legs, and will help maintain your momentum into the slope.

When you do change down from the large to the small ring on the front it is important to change this first and then

The wrong combination: hitting a climb in 'large to large' means a major shift to the small frontring is inevitable.

make any change to the rear immediately afterwards in order to maintain the same pressure on the pedals to keep your momentum. So practise downshifting into an easier gear as you come to a stop or begin the approach to a big hill.

Ease the pressure on your pedals slightly when changing gear in a climb: the force applied to the chain when climbing can be massive, so help your bike and ease the change of gear by 'pausing' your leg effort for a split second as you make the change – this is especially important if you are changing up a gear to gain more speed, or are out of the saddle and need to change down. It is easy to jump the chain off, and if you are on a steep climb, this can make it difficult to re-mount the bike after putting the chain back on. Ask Andy Schleck about this, and you might get an interesting comment after the events on the Bales climb in the 2010 Tour. As a matter of interest, we have ridden that climb several times, and it really is as steep as it looked as his chain jumped off the chainring …

Shift Often

As the hill continues or gets steeper, continue to shift to keep your cadence in a range that is comfortable. By shifting to progressively smaller gears you break up the work on your body into stable periods, allowing your heart rate and fatigue to adjust.

Avoid Cross-Chaining

It's hard on your chain and your sprockets to be at extreme angles. To avoid this, don't shift your bike to a spot where it's on the smallest ring in the front and the smallest gear in the back – or vice versa, on the large ring in both front and back. That puts the chain on opposite extreme ends of the spectrum, and if you find yourself in this situation, it's time for a big shift in the front gear to help synchronize things again.

Listen to More Experienced Riders

Pay attention as to when, and to what gear other riders are changing as you approach, and during, a climb. You can learn

Aero-tuck position for a non-professional, enthusiastic amateur!

from the way they conserve energy and use their gears to optimize the effort – especially with regard to not going too hard, too early, and thus 'running out of steam' as the climb progresses. Selecting the right gear at the right time is critical to this. The best climbers – or 'grimpeurs' as they are known – usually change down early in a climb and spin rather than pound a big gear as the slope gets steeper.

Don't Coast Down the Other Side

Once you are over the top, shift to a higher gear in order to maintain your momentum and maximize your speed on the descent. Be careful not to push too hard a gear too early on the descent because you want your legs to recover from the effort, but do use the opportunity to push your advantage home for the hard effort of your climb. Keep pedalling down the hill, even if not actually driving the bike forwards harder, as this will also help to disperse the lactic acid which will have accumulated during the climb a few minutes before.

Aerodynamics

Although cyclists have to overcome the forces of gravity and the rolling resistance of tyres on roads, once your speed exceeds around 25km/h, it is aerodynamic drag that becomes the main enemy. The one free way to go faster without pedalling harder or training for longer is to adapt your position to minimize drag.

In scientific terms, drag is a frictional force caused by the turbulence of displaced air that is pushed out of the way as you pass through it. Pedalling along at 32km/h requires the displacement of no less than 450kg of air per minute – and the fact is that the human body was not designed that well for cutting through air on a bike. This is the reason why professional teams now use Formula 1 wind tunnels to test bikes and bike position aerodynamics in order to make marginal improvements. Over the course of a long event, even a small improvement in aerodynamics pays big dividends.

If you are not riding for a professional cycling team, you don't have to worry about being able to adopt the flat-backed, low-tuck style that they use – that position is probably beyond most of us. However, small changes can reap rewards, so work at your position and you will see a difference in your speeds and the amount of energy you use. As we have said, greater benefits can arise not only from riding low over the top tube, but also from adopting a tucked-in, narrower profile on the bike, just like a time triallist. Your position on the bike will be determined by the terrain and conditions that you ride in, but maintaining an aerodynamic position will be very useful in saving energy over the length of a sportive.

Keep yourself as compact and narrow as possible.

Because energy-sapping aerodynamic drag is always present when cycling, learning how to minimize drag is vital for speed. Studies show that around one third of drag is caused by the bike, and two-thirds by the rider, so reducing rider drag is the number one priority. The best way to achieve this is to hone your riding position such that you can deliver your maximum power with minimum drag.

The Optimal Riding Position

The optimum riding position will depend on the type of bike being ridden, but below are some of the best ways to reduce drag:

- Try and keep the torso relatively flat, but certainly no more than at a 45-degree angle to the top tube. Ensure that you haven't flattened to the extent that your knees

Riding with your hands on the drops adds speed.

hit your stomach or ribcage at the top of the pedal movement. Keep the elbows tucked in, and the shoulders curved into as aerodynamic a profile as you can manage – comfortably. It is important to practise riding in a more aerodynamic position – if you don't, then you may not be training your muscles to support any sustained period of riding in that position. On balance, however, don't compromise comfort and breathing for the sake of a sleeker position

- Whenever possible get down on to the drops (the flat part of the handlebars), as this can see your speed increase by up to 2 or 3km/h; this can save you considerable energy, especially when riding on your own or in smaller groups. If we were to rank the top ten technique faults we observe in sportive riders, then not using the drops enough would be up at the top. Over the course of a 160km ride, dropping down on to the hooks of the handlebars as often as possible can, and will, save energy and time

- Ensure the knees stay close to the bike frame, and don't splay outwards. When descending, 'grip' the top tube with your knees to keep the smallest frontal area possible

Try to balance your weight evenly on long descents.

- Tuck down on the drop handlebars and adopt a 3 and 9 o'clock position with the feet on the pedals during long descents
- Clothing can make a big difference to the amount of drag experienced. The lowest drag clothing is both tight-fitting and has a low 'surface drag' as the air flows over it. At the very least ensure you wear a snug-fitting top, and that any wind or rain jackets do not flap around due to being too big. All regular cyclists are at some point teased for being lycra fetishists, but there is good reason for wearing the material: it is light, durable and aerodynamic.

Minimizing drag requires a combination of correct rider position, riding tactics and equipment. The first two strategies are cheap – a simple drop in stem height or spending more time on the drops can knock minutes off your time.

On the other hand, going 'aero' with your bike and its components could cost hundreds or even thousands of pounds. However, never lose sight of the fact that while reducing drag is a worthwhile goal, it shouldn't be at the expense of building a strong cycling engine. Remember, it is power that you need to overcome drag, and building your leg muscles and power output will have a dramatic effect on your overall performance.

Malcolm Elliott, now approaching fifty and still at the top of UK cycling, stresses the importance he places on leg work in the gym: he does several sessions a week and believes this is as important as being out there on the bike as part of his training regime. We would argue that building leg power and reducing some body fat will make much more difference to the average sportive rider's performance than spending money on ever lighter components for the bike.

Tackling Climbing

More than any other part of riding, the ability to climb well defines your performance over a sportive. Clearly, the key to climbing quickly is your power-to-weight ratio – the lighter you are, or the more power you produce, the faster you will rise up hills and mountains … or not. For those of us who are not 60kg 'grimpeurs', the way we tackle climbs can make a huge difference to our enjoyment, pace and recovery during a ride.

Different techniques are required for short, sharp, UK-style climbs as opposed to the longer mountain passes typically found in European events. It is easy to underestimate UK sportives as few have the length of climbs found in the Pyrenees or the Alps (often up to 30km), but UK climbs tend to be short and sharp and can sap energy in a different way. One of the most challenging aspects of many UK sportives is that hills rise suddenly and steeply out of relatively flat areas, and just as suddenly level off again. This can be very tiring, as this type of terrain breaks up a rider's rhythm and creates fluctuations in style and effort.

Tackling Hills

Any long training ride will involve hills, and it is easy to avoid them if you don't enjoy them. But although few people enjoy climbing, the key is to be familiar with the best way to tackle hills, and focus on the fact that the only way to enjoy exhilarating descents is to get to the top of the hill or mountain in the first place.

The best way to improve technique and speed when riding hills is to consciously go and find them, practise riding them, and get your body used to the particular riding position and stresses that come from riding uphill. Climbing need not be the all pain-inducing toil that is so often seen, as long as you follow these key rules: do not push too hard a gear; be at the front of your group; climb at an even pace; and learn how to corner uphill.

Do Not Push Too Hard a Gear

Practise riding in a low gear (34 × 25, for example). You will start improving by practising climbing at an even, fast rhythm over the length of a climb. Riding in a low gear will enable you to accelerate if required as you encounter differing gradients. If you are pushing hard against a gear too early in the climb you will build lactic acid in your legs.

Ensuring you are in the right gear early in the climb and throughout the ascent will also avoid placing undue stress

Just think of the downhill to come!

As you approach a climb, position yourself at the front of the group.

on your equipment, as attempting to change up a gear whilst climbing places a huge load on your gears. This is especially true for changing from the larger front chainring to the smaller ring. If you know or can see the profile of the climb is going to require a drop to the lower gears, then change down on to the smaller front ring before you hit the climb. If the hill is steep enough you won't miss the big chainring at all.

Be at the Front of Your Group

When riding with others, try to position yourself towards the front of the group as you approach a climb. This will ensure that even if you are not the fastest climber in the group, although you will move backwards through the group as the climb progresses you will still be with it towards the top.

One detail of technique to note: as a rider gets up out of the saddle on a slope, it is quite common for them to slow down slightly before picking up momentum again. In that split second, if you happen to be too close to their back wheel, you can clash wheels and one or both riders will fall. So watch out for the rider who is ahead of you, and stay clear of his or her back wheel. Also, learn to drive forwards

as you yourself rise out of the saddle to avoid the possibility of a clash.

There is nothing more demotivating than being on the back of a group and dropping out of touch as the group accelerates into the distance. Your mind needs to play a very strong role in making your body react to stop this happening. The fact is that usually you are perfectly able to stay with the pace even if it hurts for a short distance; during an event, every rider will feel pain at some point, and every rider will go through mini crises. You have to learn to deal with these as they happen, and ride through them. Your training sessions should incorporate routines to help you build the capability to accelerate suddenly to hang on to a group, and these sessions can often take the form of unstructured training like 'fartlek', in which you each take turns to accelerate without warning and sprint for lamp posts, trees, road signs and so on.

If, however, the pace is just too hot and you do drop back, don't panic or push too deep into your reserves to catch up again, and particularly not early in a climb or at an early stage of the event – ride at your own threshold and trust your ability to re-group on the descent. If all else fails, then simply wait for another group to come along, when the chances are you'll be one of the stronger members of this second group anyway.

Sit back on the saddle with your hands on top of the bars.

Climb At An Even Pace

As you approach a climb it is important to prepare mentally and physically for the next phase of the ride. From a physical perspective it is important to breathe deeply both through your nose and mouth – that technique will help to lower your heart rate as much as possible. By breathing very deeply and slowly, and pausing before exhaling, it is possible to lower your heart rate by a few beats per minute.

The most efficient way to climb is to maintain an even pace. Changes in pace can waste energy and take you beyond your threshold, so it is important to settle into your own pace, one that you can maintain from the base to the top of the climb. At this point let us emphasize something that has been said in several different contexts: successful sportive riding, or indeed success in any endurance activity, is all about executing the performance at your own pace, and not trying to follow others or do as they do. Certainly it's quite all right to chase a group in order to gain some recovery from riding with them, or to speed up at certain points of the event, but the quickest way to blow up or fail to achieve a good result is to try to ride someone else's event. Riders who charge off are invariably overhauled

toward the end of an event. So pace yourself according to your own ability and thresholds.

On short climbs it is acceptable to go beyond your threshold if it means being able to stay with a group that you have been riding with, but our experience shows that you are better riding your own pace, conserving energy and trusting your ability to close the gap as you go down the other side.

Technique For Cornering Uphill

On steep climbs you may well encounter hairpin bends that are much steeper towards the inside of the bend than the outside. Rather than wasting effort by taking the shortest line, which would include clipping the apex at the steepest point, it is best to ride the widest possible line around the shallowest part of the corner. A single corner may not save you much energy, but the cumulative effect on a long climb can save you a lot. Remember to look beyond the corner and up the climb for other cyclists descending or cars heading down the hill – and unless you are in a closed road event, stay on your own side of the road.

Optimal Position For Climbing

The most efficient position to climb is to stay seated with your hands resting on top of the bars and your backside towards the back of your saddle. This position places your weight over the rear wheel, takes weight off the front of the bike, and helps you engage your gluteal muscles – the largest muscle group in the body – to maximize your power during the climb.

Tests on riding in the saddle as opposed to out of the saddle have shown that your heart rate is lower at the same power output whilst seated than if you get out of the saddle, although some riders still favour an out-of-the-saddle style. If that is how you like to ride instinctively, then make sure you incorporate specific out-of-saddle training sessions on climbs in order to familiarize yourself with the quadricep muscle pain that often accompanies these efforts. If you can develop a high cadence spinning, seated style, then this will pay dividends, and you can keep the out-of-saddle efforts for catching a group or powering over the top of a climb.

Out-Of-Saddle Climbing Technique

On very steep sections of a climb you may simply be forced to stand up on your pedals to maximize your power for a short period. Equally, on longer, shallow climbs, it is a good idea to periodically change up a gear and get out of the saddle to stretch your legs and move position. You only need to stand up for perhaps 100 metres, but this will stop you feeling stiff and will help stretch your back.

If you do need to stand, then transfer from the seated position by gently transferring your weight forwards as you come out of the saddle. Remember that as you stand you will be pushing greater force through the pedals so you may need to change up a gear. Changing gear will give you a slightly more stable platform on which to pedal, and will also allow you the flexibility of changing back down as the gradient increases or you become a little more tired. If you are standing and need to change up a gear, then when you return to the saddle change back down a gear to maintain the same cadence.

Before you transfer from sitting to standing, move your hands to the top of the brake hoods and hook your index finger under the hood towards the top of the brake lever. Focus on pulling up on the hoods as you climb (mentally picture yourself trying to keep the front wheel as light as possible and pulling it up the slope). Pushing your weight down through your arms on to the front wheel as you climb will slow your progress and lead to tiredness. Some people envisage climbing in this way as climbing up the rungs of a ladder, which might be a useful image to hold in your head.

It is important when you are riding out of the saddle not to rock the bike too far either side as you pedal, but to sway it slightly and use your bodyweight to generate greater downward force. As you become stronger (especially through core exercises such as crunches) your stability will improve because your upper legs will have a stronger 'platform' to push against. However, when the gradient gets really steep or you are tired towards the end of an event, you may need to muster all your energy simply to keep the pedals turning, in which case the extra leverage afforded from rocking the bike can help transfer power during the downward pedal stroke.

Hooking your hands under the bars allows you to pull up if you come out of the saddle.

Stand for greater power, but stay relaxed.

Keep the bike stable.

Over the Top

So you have reached the top of the climb in decent shape and without pushing too far into the red, and are looking forward to the next part of the ride. Once you have reached the top of the climb you must take time to recover from the effort and prepare your body and mind for the next phase of the event. In the UK where there are many short, steep climbs it is important to keep pedalling over the brow of any climb to spin your legs and dissipate any lactate acid build-up.

Similarly on the descent: even if the descent is steep, it's important to keep turning your legs over and ride the lactate from the previous climb out of your muscles. If you descend and immediately face another climb without turning your pedals you will not have recovered, and the next climb will feel like a continuation of the first. If lactate builds up in your muscles, eventually it will inhibit the chemical process that provides fuel for muscles to operate effectively, and you will cramp or grind to a halt.

The likelihood is that you will be hot and potentially dehydrated, so take time to drink. For a long descent, especially after European climbs, you may well choose to put on a lightweight gilet or jacket at the top of the climb, as a high speed descent can be a very cold experience.

NUTRITION/HYDRATION

Drinking and eating during a climb can be difficult, especially if you are riding at or over your threshold, but it is critical to eat and drink on the longer climbs found in Europe, where it is quite possible that a climb will last for over two hours and cover over 20km. For these climbs it is important to ensure you have enough fluids to last the climb, so if there is a food stop or water fountain available at the base then take the time to stop and fill your bottles.

When riding in mainland Europe it is quite common for villages to have a drinking tap or spring (most likely near the village square) so you can always find water. Drinking and eating small amounts at regular intervals (every 15 minutes for fluids, every 30 minutes for food/fuel) will help keep you hydrated and your energy levels consistent. Small amounts are more easily digestible and easier to chew and swallow as the lungs heave and the breath is forced from between clenched teeth on the steepest parts of the hill.

It is obvious, perhaps, but try to coincide food and fluid intake with stretches of the climb that flatten out slightly. Another small but surprisingly useful tip from experience is to cut the tops off your energy bars before the event so that they slide out quickly and easily when required. (Don't do this with gels, for obvious reasons....) Many riders struggle to bite the top off a bar wrapper while trying to maintain an easy breathing rhythm.

Long, hard climbs can turn into a solitary experience!

Cornering and Descending

Cornering and descending are placed together here because the techniques are essentially an extension of one another; the main difference is the distribution of your weight towards the back of the bike as you enter a corner on a descent. Having conquered a climb you must descend at some point – even though, from bitter experience, some events don't feel like that. Descending fast, in control, and overtaking fellow riders is one of the most exhilarating feelings in a sportive. However, if you do not have the right technique and therefore the confidence to let the bike flow, you will dread descending, and will subsequently harm your chances of competing successfully and gaining maximum enjoyment from the ride.

Your speed on exiting a corner determines your speed along the following section of road or the effort required to reach that speed – 5km/h faster out of a corner can mean being 15 to 20km/h quicker down the next section and into the next corner. When you repeat this on a long descent the cumulative effect you can gain over a more cautious

rider can translate into a five or ten minute advantage. It is very difficult for anyone to make up that much time on the flat or the next climb, so maximizing your speed on the entry, apex and exit of corners is both satisfying and a very worthwhile skill to practise.

Knowing that you are able to descend fast has the added bonus of relaxing you during a climb. Other riders may ride away from you, but you can relax knowing that unless they also excel downhill, the likelihood is that you will re-join them on the descent. So, this section is intended to be a reference point to enable you to learn key techniques that will help you descend faster with lower risk.

Reading the Road Ahead

At the risk of sounding obvious, a key way to increase your speed through a corner or down a descent is to look ahead. If you are nervous you will tend to grip the handlebars tightly and only concentrate on the road immediately in front of you, which will do nothing to calm your fears or help you relax, as you will be constantly reacting to changes in road direction, camber, condition and other riders.

As you approach a corner there are a number of clues that can help you determine which way the road goes, the severity of the bend, and any hazards that might lie ahead. It is very important that you remain constantly aware of other riders, especially in sportives where there may be thousands of participants, as the variation in ability will be very wide and this can lead to actions by other people that appear illogical. Give yourself space, and remember that you have little to gain from following another rider's wheel on a descent.

An example of reading the road is coming over the top of a climb and seeing a number of hairpin bends on the descent. This affords a great opportunity to look ahead and down the mountain to assess the road and start to plan your approach for each corner. Equally, on wooded descents the tree line or flow of a river can give you the direction of the next corner.

Make sure you can see clearly for your full expected braking distance. If you cannot stop within the distance you can see, then gently apply the front brake to slow your speed to a level that gives you confidence to stop. Your mind needs to be working faster than the speed of your bike, and you can't do that if you're looking only 10 metres ahead of your front wheel, or you turn into a bend

too early and can't see what's round the corner. We learned the technique of looking at the exit of the bend rather than the bend itself in our earlier lives racing cars at circuits such as Spa, the Nurburgring and Silverstone, where focusing on the exit point makes a big difference to both line through the bend and exit speed.

It is always important to concentrate on the farthest point you can see down the road, and then scan back to where you are. Observe where the road in the distance converges to a single point (the vanishing point), and watch the direction in which it turns.

The Four Phases of a Corner

There are four distinct elements to cornering: the entry, braking, turn-in and exit. It is your ability to connect the four phases into a seamless flow that will determine your speed through the bend and along the next section.

The Entry

As you approach a corner you should be fully aware of who and what is around you. Be aware of the other riders with you, and always be careful of riders coming inside you on turns. Undertaking (passing on a rider's inside line) is mas-

Come into the corner having pre-selected your gear to match your exit speed.

Apply the front brake in a straight line.

sively irritating and incredibly dangerous to both the rider doing the undertaking and the rider being passed. It is an unwritten rule in sportives never to overtake on the inside of a rider. The person undertaking on the inside is often inexperienced or out of control, and what starts as a massively impressive pro-like dart for the inside line all too often ends with a wide exit across the line of other riders. This has the inevitable consequence of riders falling and being injured, through no fault of their own.

If you do come up behind a rider as you enter the corner, wait for them to hit the apex of the curve and start their exit before telling them that you will be coming through on their outside (shout 'On your right' if you are in the UK or 'On your left' if you are in Europe); this way they know you are there, and can move over after coming through the corner safely.

As you approach the corner look ahead to the road surface and notice if there are white lines or loose gravel on the outside or the inside of turn. These must be avoided, particularly in wet conditions, so it is better to take a different line at the expense of speed than risk braking or turning on what are both potentially very slippery features.

Is it dry? Are there any loose bits? Which way is the camber? Is it downhill? Can you see the exit? Many factors affect your decision on how the corner is taken, at what speed and from which angle.

In the entry phase of a corner you should position your bike a foot in from the kerb, look as far along the road as you can see, then scan back to where you are. You are about to brake very hard and need to make sure the road surface is up to it.

Change down a gear, as that will help you exit the corner as quickly as possible. This will become second nature with experience. The old motor-racing maxim of 'slow in, fast out' remains very true in cycling. 'Fast in' usually means slow out, or will require you to alter your line in mid-corner, which will slow you down or could put other riders at risk. Being in the right gear will help you save energy when 'accelerating' out of the corner.

Braking

Once in the correct gear to exit the corner, it's time to brake. Be sure not to grab, snatch or jam on the brakes, but apply both sets of pads quickly but smoothly to the rims, feel them bite, then gently but forcibly apply the front brake. Note that most of your braking effort will take place at the front end, even though you are applying even pressure on the levers; during a fast descent your bodyweight will be pushing towards the front and the rear end will be very light, thus requiring relatively little braking to slow it down. It is important to understand the dynamics involved, because getting them wrong at 70 or even 90km/h can be very challenging....

It's important to do all your braking in a straight line if at all possible, because this will minimize the risk of your rear wheel coming out of line, or understeering with a locked front wheel.

As you brake, the weight of you and the bike immediately transfers to the front wheel. What was a previous 45/55 front-to-rear weight balance has now gone to 70/30, if not 80/20 on a downhill, or even 90/10 on a sharp hairpin bend. As the bike and rider's weight transfers and the forces of inertia cause it to become unstable, the ability to grip the road increases but you enter the most dangerous part of the corner. Anything that happens from here on in is a direct consequence of your own actions, so do everything gently.

Once you start braking, the front wheel is now much more capable of handling even more braking force, and the rear wheel less so; in some cases you can brake so hard you can feel the rear lift from the ground. To prevent this, and to keep your bike in as stable a state as possible, slide your backside backwards on the saddle to keep the rear wheel in place.

The back brake is used to stabilize the rear end and stop it coming round. With your backside over the back wheel you've dramatically increased its capacity to grip and re-established a 60/40 weight distribution.

On long, fast descents with many corners it is possible that your brake pads and rims will get very hot, which means their ability to grip dramatically increases. So gently ease the brakes off to stop them grabbing. A hot wheel requires a lot less 'pull' on the brakes than a cold wheel does to generate the same braking force. If you hold the same amount of 'pull' on the brakes all the way up to the corner turn-in, you risk a front wheel locking.

On the subject of 'pull', no two riders are the same in terms of their preferred tension on the brake cables; some prefer to have to pull the levers a fair way before they engage, and some like them to engage instantly. Whichever style suits you, remember that you need to be able to apply full 'pull' using a maximum of two fingers around the lever, and preferably one, thereby allowing your hands to exert maximum control on the handlebars in tricky situations.

As you reach the turn-in you should be looking to find the exit of the corner and nothing else. When you see the exit of the corner you need to focus on a smooth transition into the turn and start to re-shift your weight forwards again by moving your backside forwards on the saddle.

Keep your weight up, come off the brakes, and turn in.

The Turn-In

Do not be tempted to turn in too early. Too many people turn in to a corner far too early, and this is probably one of the biggest mistakes made by amateur riders. By turning in too early you limit your options, minimize possible escape strategies, compromise your view of obstacles, and potentially place both yourself and other riders in danger. There is no advantage whatsoever to turning early into a corner during a sportive – you are not protecting your race position.

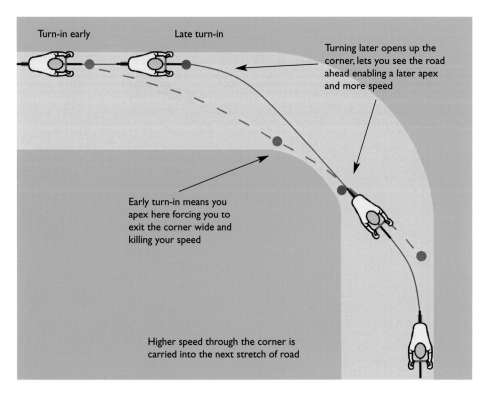

Turn-in early   Late turn-in

Turning later opens up the corner, lets you see the road ahead enabling a later apex and more speed

Early turn-in means you apex here forcing you to exit the corner wide and killing your speed

Higher speed through the corner is carried into the next stretch of road

LEFT: The correct line for safer, faster cornering.

BELOW: The ideal technique mid-corner.

The instant you see the exit, you should release both brakes at exactly the same rate, gently and with purpose. Don't destabilize the bike by rushing it, and move your hands away from the brakes.

As you release the brakes the weight begins to unload from the front, which is undesirable: if you remember, your backside is hanging over the back of the saddle, which in effect lifts the front wheel from the ground. The front needs to grip to turn in, so that's where you need your weight. As you release the brakes, slide your backside forwards to get the weight balance back toward the front wheel.

The front is the part that needs grip to get you round the corner, so you need to 'push' the front into the ground. Try to remain relaxed while you do this – focus on placing the palms of your hands on the bars, rather than wrestling them with a death grip. Don't forget that it isn't just the tyre surface that is keeping you upright and allowing you to manoeuvre at high speed through bends; as your wheels spin you are creating a downward force, which is the main reason for being able to grip the road with your tyres. (It's incredible to think that all this control and contact comes from approximately 8 to 10mm of tyre/road surface contact, if you use a standard 23mm tyre.)

Lean in to the bike and relax your shoulders over the bars. Get your outside crank at the six o'clock position, and push down hard with your outside leg. Lift your backside just slightly, perhaps 2–3mm off the saddle to help ensure you're doing it properly.

COUNTER STEERING

Most people will turn their bike right by pushing the left hand forwards and pulling the right hand back towards them. In fact this is the exact opposite of how to turn quickly, effectively and safely. Counter steering is the technique used by the best descenders to corner at speed.

To demonstrate what we mean by this, do the following exercise: accelerate the bike up to 16km/h in the centre of the road and stop pedalling. As you slowly roll forwards, with your hands on the drops, open your palms so the thumb is on the inside of the bar and your fingers are on the outside. Your fingers should be parallel to the ground with only the palm in contact with the bars.

Gently push down and away from yourself at 45 degrees with your right hand. Your bike will move to the right very quickly. Do the same to the other side, and you will go left. The harder you push away from you, the quicker the bike will turn.

As you get more experienced and confident with counter steering you can get the bike to turn very quickly – it will turn through 45 degrees almost within its own length. The sooner you get the tyre on its shoulder, the faster, better and safer the bike will corner: one of the main reasons why people have difficulty in cornering is because they don't get the tyre on its shoulder. That's where the grip is, and that's where the circumference of the tyre is less, making it turn in a tighter arc than it would on its crown.

Point your inside knee to the corner apex to help the turn-in, and look at nothing else but as far down the exit road as you can. Pick a tree, gate or lamp post that's as far away as you can see, but has a direct line of sight between you and where you want to be, and stay focused on it.

The Exit

Once you've got the bike on its side you will be able to see the exit fully and where you need to be. If there is any obstruction in the road don't look at it, as your bike will follow your eyes. If you have your escape route planned you should have plenty of room, and the last thing you want to do is aim inexorably at some random debris or obstacle that could trip you up.

Look as far down the road as you can, and pick up a landmark: the bike will track straight for it. You can now begin to restore the bike to its upright position by gently rising out of the saddle and beginning to get on top of the gears. Keep looking down the road – there is nothing behind you to help you – and never look back: there is no point, and most riders who turn have a tendency to move off line as they do so, thereby moving them into the path of another rider, or worse, an oncoming vehicle.

Remember, you turned in late and fast, which gets the bike through the corner in half the time and allows you to begin your exit phase sooner. You've also given yourself advance warning of any issues that may arise, and have given yourself the time to deal with them. Also, you have

made your exit parallel to the wall, sheer drop, oncoming traffic, or the trees on the outside, and are not heading straight for them as an early turner-in would be, who is now probably hard on the brakes.

Choose your exit: don't let it be dictated to you by nerves, bad planning, or circumstances you have not anticipated.

The sooner you can get back to full power, the sooner you begin to capitalize on your gained time, and the sooner the bike gets you back on to the next straight.

Riding in a Group

By mastering the art of riding with others you could save a third of your energy and ride faster for longer. One of the most exhilarating feelings when riding in a sportive is rolling through beautiful countryside as part of a large group (a peloton). This is the closest many of us will get to feeling like a professional cyclist operating for a long distance at close to the speed that the pro peloton rides at. However, this can also be a scary and intimidating experience for the novice, as perhaps for the first time you become very dependent on the behaviour, experience and capability of other riders. And on a longer ride, this dependency on the competence and awareness of others can be mentally draining as well.

Riding in a group is easier and faster than riding on your own, so mastering the technique, understanding the rules, and learning how to communicate, will really improve your performance and enjoyment. As sportives have grown in popularity the number of riders attracted to these events has risen considerably. This rise has predominantly come from riders attracted to the sport through fitness goals, but often without the opportunity to ride as part of a group other than in an event. Indeed, you may be part of the 70 per cent of sportive riders who are not members of a

CONFIDENCE

The first big problem with cornering and descending at speed is that it becomes addictive. The second big problem is complacency. To corner fast you need to concentrate, and the moment you stop concentrating you and those around you are in danger, and sooner or later you will crash.

The payback for all this concentration is that you corner with less stress, and burn far less nervous energy, than those for whom every corner is a tribulation. In other words you actually save yourself energy and go quicker at the same time.

The confidence that descending gives you is a great leveller. You know you can let others drift away from you on the climbs if you have to, especially in the last few kilometres, because you can get them back on the descent. In a 100-mile sportive, every ounce of energy saved is a bonus, and when you save energy you build confidence in your ability to push hard in the latter part of an event.

cycling club and who cover many hundreds or thousands of relatively solitary training miles as they prepare for their chosen events.

One of the real benefits of a cycling club is the opportunity to ride with others in a group and learn the skills required to ride safely and predictably. If you can manage to organize your schedule and plan sessions with others, then joining a local club is a great way to learn skills and hone fitness.

While you might enter a sportive with a friend or group, you will predominantly be riding alongside riders that you don't know. This makes it even more important that you understand the etiquette, signals and language so you can add to the strength of the group. Fortunately the language of group riding is common across international boundaries, so time invested will be well spent.

The Key Principles of Group Riding

Before considering the signals, language and technique, it is important to understand the key principles of group riding; these might be described as doing your bit; not being a hero; riding smoothly; not half-wheeling; communicating; following the wheel; looking ahead; knowing your limits; and being courteous.

Doing your bit: If you want to benefit from the collective efforts of the group you must be prepared to do your share of the work – no one likes a 'wheel sucker', the term for a rider who sits sheltering behind everyone, doing no work but getting the benefit of reduced wind drag.

Don't be a hero: While you may be the strongest rider in a group, don't get carried away and spend too much time on the front. Conserve your energy. This will also serve to increase the average speed of the group, as the lead riders are not given the time to tire through spending too long pulling the group along.

Another major technique error we see in sportives is riders taking too long a 'pull' at the front of a group; this is unnecessary, and it is also counterproductive, as it wears them out and the overall pace of the group falls. The key is to keep the lead rider changing all the time; we would usually ride for no longer than a minute or two at the front before drifting gently back through the group for a recovery phase.

Half-wheeling is dangerous for both riders.

Follow the wheel in front to maximize 'pull' from the lead rider.

Be smooth: Sudden change can be dangerous, so always be aware, and brake, turn, swerve and accelerate in moderation.

Don't half-wheel: If you ride half way up a fellow rider's wheel you run the risk of collision if they need to come off their line to avoid a hazard. Stay fully alongside or fully behind.

Communicate: No rider is a mind reader, so if in doubt... shout (and signal).

Follow the wheel: Be consistent through the group in riding the same distance from the rider in front. If you see gaps open beyond two or three bike lengths, this can lead to the group splitting, or wasted energy in closing down the gap.

Look ahead: This sounds obvious, but it is easy to become transfixed on the wheel in front of you. Try to look up and ahead to read the road and anticipate the movement of your fellow riders.

Know your limits: Remember that you are riding for 160km, so be careful not to get carried away too early.

Riding in a group is great, but not if you are above your threshold. Be prepared to back off, ride to your own pace, and wait for the next group behind to come along.

Be courteous: Simple manners can get you a long way – donning lycra does not mean you are excused. Nose-blowing, eating and drinking is best saved for when you are positioned at the rear of the group.

Simply being aware of these principles will positively enhance your experience in a sportive. Sportive riders are not always the 'best behaved' cyclists: perhaps because they lack group riding experience they often ignore cycling's basic etiquette and act as if they are the only riders on the road. Try to take some time to learn and practise the basic rules of the cycling road; you will ride more comfortably, more safely and probably faster for it.

Language and Signals

It is important to let those riding behind you know what is coming up ahead, or what you are planning to do. In a larger group you must remember that people towards the rear of the group are relying on you for their safety.

Be careful not to shout too frequently, as this can make the group nervous. When you ride in European sportives remember that not everyone will speak English, and sudden calls, if not clear, can cause sudden braking or changes in direction that can easily cause a pile-up, or 'chute' as it's known to the pro riders.

The following are the most common shouts within a group, what they mean, and how you should react:

'**Car on**': Car approaching, take care; go into single file if on a narrow road.

'**Car up**': Car behind; move to single file and allow it to pass.

'**Clear**': As you approach a junction, check for traffic: if it is clear, then give a positive shout of 'clear'.

'**Last man**': As someone moves off the front to the rear of the group, if you are last in line then shout this as he or she comes alongside you to let them know that they can come in behind you.

'**Stop**': If you arrive at a junction but the road is not clear, then shout 'Stop' to pre-warn other riders.

The easiest way to communicate among a group is to use signals. The following are the most common problems, and the signals you should use, or might expect to see, that would give warning of them:

Punctures/problems with your bike: Raise your hand directly in the air to warn others you will be slowing down. Pull over to the verge when safe.

Come through: A flick of the elbow (outwards and away from your body) on the side that you want riders to come through. This indicates that you have done your work and you are about to slow and allow riders to come through before taking your place at the back of the line.

A clear signal for a following rider to come through.

Clearly point to the pothole or debris to be avoided.

Wave away from the hazard, indicating the direction to move out.

Pothole or debris: If you come upon a pothole or debris in the road then point down towards the hazard to indicate its presence to others, and warn them you may be moving out to avoid it.

Moving out: If you see a hazard ahead such as a parked car, speed bump or manhole cover that you need to avoid, indicate that you will be moving out from the gutter, and for others to follow, by 'wafting' your left hand behind your back in a waving motion.

Coming into the line: You will need to use this signal if you are riding two abreast and hear a shout warning of a car approaching from ahead or behind, or if you are coming down the line after your turn on the front and other riders are not strong enough to maintain the line. If this happens and you want to come into the line at a certain point, then point to the rear wheel of the bike that you want to follow and say 'Coming in'. Wait for acknowledgement from the rider you want to come in front of, wait for the gap to open, and then pull into the line.

Slow down: If you see a junction or hazard ahead, then sit up and move your hand to the side, palm down, and complete a 'patting' motion as you slow down.

Riding Efficiently

As a consequence of the effect of wind resistance, riding behind another rider uses significantly less effort. So a key element in saving energy is to ride with other riders balancing your time on the front with time spent resting in the group. If the group starts pulling away, don't destroy yourself trying to stay in touch. As we said earlier, in a sportive you are better off conserving your energy and waiting for the next group behind to come through so you can ride along with them instead.

On the flat, pedal smoothly and efficiently, and if you do have to get out of the saddle, say for a short climb, try your utmost not to slow down or shoot your bike backwards as you stand up.

One of the biggest mistakes riders make is over-reacting to hazards, either ones they've spotted or had pointed out. Just remember that there will be people riding as close to you as you are to the rider in front. So don't haul on the

Pat your hand up and down if you intend to slow down.

anchors, but feather your brakes and try not to make any sudden movements. The further back you are in a chain gang, group or peloton, the less time you are likely to have to react.

'Le Patron'

In an event you will come across many different styles of riding and personalities. If you don't care for these, remember that you can always drop off the group and wait for the next one to come along – or if you are stronger, ride away.

If you are riding an event with a group of friends, or if you join up with others on the road, it can be useful to assign a leader (termed a 'patron' by the pros) for the group. He is then responsible for pace, when to change the lead rider smoothly, accelerating away from junctions, adding new members to the line, and on a very long ride, all the other necessary stops and pauses that have to occur.

The 'patron' can also play a key part in organizing others to join and work with you; do not be afraid to ask other riders if they want to be an active rider in the group. Be clear that if they are prepared to work and 'do their bit', then they are more than welcome – but if they are not, then indicate that they should ride alone.

Our experience has shown that it is often difficult to maintain a controlled group of more than eight riders. If you do come across a rider asking you if you want to work together, then grasp the opportunity and enjoy the ride.

We have ridden many long sportives over distances ranging from 100 to 550km, and at the longer end of these, being able to move in with groups and ride conservatively with others can mean the difference between finishing and dropping out. It's an incredibly tough thing, both physically and mentally, to ride a long event totally solo, and to achieve your best time as well is a big challenge. It's perfectly acceptable and often enjoyable to ride with others and work together, so learn the skills and take advantage of the bonus it provides.

Be clear with your intent to move in.

Experience Says …

- Pace yourself on a climb – take into account its length and severity, and make sure you do not go too hard, too early, as you will not have a chance to recover
- Find your own pace, do not be influenced by others, and aim to ride a climb at the same even pace over its entirety
- Alternate your position – in order to stay supple, try to alter your position between seated and standing on the bike at regular intervals
- Change up a gear before you need to get out of the saddle. You can lose momentum if you do not do this
- Keep pedalling – at the top of a climb keep pedalling over the top to remove lactic acid from your legs. This goes for the descent as well

- Stay loose when descending – loose hands, look ahead, do not feather the brakes
- Beware gaps in hedges – a side wind can blow you off line
- When taking a corner, judge your turn-in point and then turn one or two metres after that point in order to give yourself greater margin for error on the exit
- Avoid white lines, especially in the wet, as the smooth surface of white paint can be incredibly slippery
- If you find yourself carrying too much speed into a corner, shift your weight back by sliding to the rear of the saddle, then brake hard in a straight line with the front brake first and then with a 70:30 front/rear bias
- Do not be afraid of not turning at all and coming to a stop – better to be stopped than on your backside
- Do not be a hero when riding in a group. Do your bit, listen to your riding partners, and always beware of the impact your actions can have on others.

CHAPTER 7

RIDE WITH YOUR MIND

Sooner or later, halfway up a 9 per cent climb, or 80 miles in with 20 to go, this is going to hurt. Every sportive rider experiences rough patches; it's a tough sport and sportives are arduous events that challenge both body and mind. You are probably used to your legs hurting a bit, having a stiff neck, or aches and pains in your lower back, but if you haven't ridden many long-distance bike events, you may not be familiar with the mental pain that is also a part of it.

You won't feel like this all the time: there will equally be periods of sublime enjoyment and satisfaction where the bike wheels skim over the smooth road surface, the wind is at your back, you eat the miles up as if they were nothing, and in every window you pass you see the reflection of a supremely toned and successful athlete.... Those moments are, as we mentioned earlier, referred to as 'la volupté' and they are rare and to be treasured.

This section looks at how to prepare the mind for the challenge of the tough sections rather than the enjoyment of the pleasant bits, and will hopefully give you a few tips and strategies for managing through those inevitable moments where you need to dig deep and keep going.

Dealing With Self Doubt

Most of us actually make things tougher than they need to be from the outset – we harbour nagging doubts about fitness, equipment, weather conditions and capability, and issues, both real and imaginary, dwell on our minds and limit our potential before we've even turned a pedal. We have all heard those voices in our heads telling us that everyone else is fitter and faster, their bikes are lighter and technically superior, and they have put in more miles.

What is both extraordinary and encouraging for the amateur sportive rider is that even the greatest riders in history experience self-doubt. Coppi, up there with the very best, was notoriously mentally fragile; Bobet, three times winner of the Tour, experienced mood swings and insecurities; and many others have revealed moments of uncertainty and fear. Today, the all-conquering British Cycling Track Squad employs a specialist adviser to work with Sir Chris Hoy and the others, preparing them for the mental challenges they face.

Somewhere inside all our heads we carry 'the worm', put there by genetics, all sorts of experiences and human frailties, and manifesting itself in different degrees – stronger or weaker – in different individuals. It gnaws away at our confidence and self-belief, and as tiredness sets in its presence grows stronger and its voice louder. It is important to develop techniques to deal with this unwelcome presence, and draw upon the reserves of positive energy and focus which have been built through all the hours and miles of training and preparation for the event.

The 'worm' attacks us in the rest of our lives as well, but fortunately most of us find that one of the positive benefits of training, competing and achieving cycling and sportive goals is to reduce the worm's influence on our lives in general, making us stronger, more determined individuals capable of dealing with issues better than before.

Developing Mental Capacity

Optimum performance in an endurance event such as a sportive can only be achieved when your three 'engines' – the bike, the body and the mind – are in harmony and are working together. So take time to learn about and understand each of them, prepare them, and set yourself up for success. To do this you need to prepare the bike, train the body and focus the mind.

There are some clear characteristics that all successful sportsmen have in their mental make-up: self-confidence, focus, self-analysis, a degree of selfishness, the ability to 'suffer' (as a cyclist would put it), willpower, self-denial, determination, optimism and a positive outlook, dedication, commitment and a refusal to be beaten or to give in. To be a successful sportive rider you will need to develop or harness your fair share of most of these attributes, and you will learn more about yourself and your mental capacity to endure than you can imagine.

But perhaps above all, a successful athlete believes in putting in enough of the right preparation and training, and uses that as the foundation for success and achievement. To ride well in a sportive, you will need to put in the mental, as well as the physical, miles. The authors are neither psychologists nor sports psychiatrists, but they have developed an understanding of how to deal with mental challenges over years of riding through the bad times, terrible weather and both physical and technical problems. There has been plenty of research, which demonstrates the link between mental preparation, toughness, focus and successful outcomes, so we all have to build mind training into our schedules as well as physical. Our personal illustration of the sequence or

The Mental Cycle

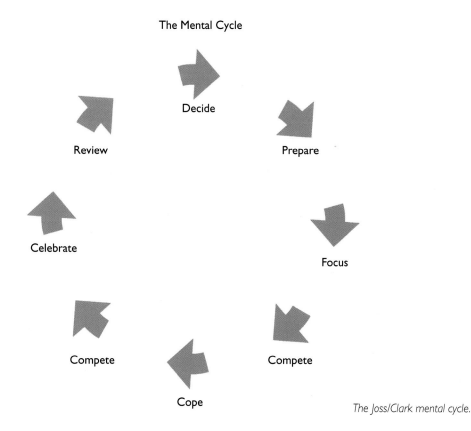

Decide

Prepare

Review

Focus

Celebrate

Compete

Compete

Cope

The Joss/Clark mental cycle.

cycle of mental states that form part of the preparation for, and execution of, a sportive is outlined above.

Deciding Your Goal

First, you decide which event you will enter – and you must also understand why you have chosen it: is it to have a fitness goal, to raise money for charity, or to change your lifestyle or introduce an element of competitive challenge into your daily routine? Are you trying to create some focal points in your fitness regime?

Whatever the reason, make sure you hold that in your mind as you begin the training programme for the event. Write the reasons down, represent them graphically, note them on your PC or whichever way suits your own style. Whatever the mechanism, make sure that when, on that cold January morning as you slog through the rain and the wind in the dark and alone, the worm starts whispering in your ear, you can summon up a clear image of why you are doing this, and send him back to where he came from.

Set up your plan, and keep the purpose and the aims clear in your mind. Decide on broad objectives, such as the time you want to achieve, and refer to these regularly as you train. Making other people aware of your objectives will help, as you will feel more peer pressure and/or support if others are involved in the build-up. Return to your objectives and aims regularly throughout the training programme to maintain a sense of purpose.

Preparing For the Event

Next you need to develop the training plan, and also organize the logistics for the event. The better and earlier you do the groundwork, both physically and logistically, the more confident you will be as you approach the event itself. Book the flights, arrange the hotel accommodation, work out what you will be taking and carrying on the bike, make sure you have read and understood all the pre-event briefing information, and then begin to prepare as you increase the training distances and intensity for the challenge ahead.

Try to incorporate several rides or lead-up events to familiarize yourself with how it feels to ride for five, six or seven hours at a time. Remember, it will hurt at some point, so experience this in advance and work out how you will deal with it when it happens. One of the key elements of training for an event is 'specificity': in other words, replicating the conditions of the event as closely as possible in training.

Focusing on the Event

Nowadays most serious athletes believe in what is called 'visualization' as part of their preparation for a major event. They will close their eyes and try to create an image of various parts of the event or activity they are about to engage in. It is important to summon up positive images of yourself feeling strong and fit, flying up the climbs or lifting your arms as you cross the finish line. Focus your mind as you draw within a month or so of the sportive on the day itself: picture yourself at the start, feeling good about why you are there, and remind yourself of the hard work you have put into the training programme. How can you fail to deliver after all this effort and careful preparation?

Finally, using a technique that we call 'mind riding', form an image of yourself at different points of the ride – maybe at the foot of a tough climb, or mentally 'turning for home' at the halfway point of the sportive. See yourself on your best bike in your event gear feeling comfortable and in control, and use this image to gain a sense of clarity and purpose as you come into the final stages of your training and preparation.

On the day of the sportive itself, clear your mind of everything superfluous to the event. You should have everything ready and you should be trained, so focus solely on the event itself and try to feel purposeful and ready.

Ready To Compete

It is essential for optimum performance to approach the start line knowing that you have done everything you can to be ready, and if you have missed something, then don't dwell on it. Now is not the time to think about what you might or might not have done differently before the ride: it's too late, and you need to make the best of where you are and what you have.

So clear your mind, and don't get caught up in other riders' agitation or angst. Stay calm, breathe deeply and slowly, and just fix on a point somewhere ahead on the course and channel your thoughts and energy positively towards that point. Try to relax, stretch gently, and once again, visualize yourself feeling strong and fit.

When you are called forwards at the start, move off steadily and confidently; don't try to race the rest of the field. A sportive is a timed event against the clock and yourself, so don't turn it into a road race – you're in the wrong place for that. In a sportive, your fellow riders are not the competition; they are there to do their best against their own objectives and goals, so while they may enhance the sense of challenge, that's as far as it should go. They are not threats to your own success; however, they can help you by working with you and sharing the workload.

Keep your game plan in the forefront of your mind, and adapt it as you need to suit conditions and how you feel.

Coping With Setbacks

When the tough moments come, as they will, it is crucial to develop 'coping' strategies to help you through them. During a long event things won't always go to plan, and you need to be able to adapt and react to how you feel, the conditions and the actions of others around you. Try to analyse things logically, remember how you got through a similar situation or problem during another event or in training, and break the problem into manageable pieces.

Stay relaxed, remain optimistic about a successful outcome, and don't make panicked decisions. Stay focused on the end goal, and make changes to your ride plan progressively over a few miles. Don't expend effort and energy on things you can't control, but move on and work on things within your own control. Commit yourself mentally to completing the event, view a setback as a temporary problem, and when you think you have given everything, there is probably still a bit more in there, so dig deeper. As Lance Armstrong famously said, 'pain is temporary, glory lasts forever'.

Be Sure To Celebrate

At the end of the sportive, don't chastise yourself, as most of us tend to do, for taking a little longer than your target time. Instead congratulate yourself on finishing your challenge and reflect back on the atmosphere, the enjoyment, and the completion of a great event.

Recall good moments when you felt strong, and those where you rode through pain or strenuous effort, and feel you have accomplished something. Let some time pass before you review the whole event and your own performance, and recover properly before attempting to analyse and play critique to your ride. When you are tired, the worm can easily make the negatives appear more substantial than the positives.

So now is the time to crack open that bottle and indulge yourself; it's back to training soon, so make the most of it today.

Reviewing the Event

Once you have recovered and rested, it is important to review various aspects of the event, particularly if you intend to ride more. Think about the event itself: was it well organized and well run on the day? Would you ride it again? How do you feel you performed on the day? What opportunities can you see to improve your time or complete the ride feeling fresher?

This is the time to adjust your training programme, and to improve the preparation you put in for the next event; you may need more mileage or more power work, or you may feel you could have tapered for the event better. Now is the time to build the lessons learned into your schedule, improve or change equipment, amend your diet or just generally reflect on a job well done.

If in the course of reviewing the event you end up concluding that you could have, maybe should have, ridden it quicker, then instead of chastising yourself, set out your goals for next time and plan to incorporate new routines or training objectives into your schedule. Keep them visible as you begin to train for the next sportive.

If you feel you made mistakes, then simply visualize correcting these as you ride the next one; above all, don't let the worm eat away and create self-doubt. Remember, you have achieved something already, which the vast majority of the population couldn't or wouldn't try, and that is something to be proud of, no matter what time you recorded.

Experience Says ...

- Prepare well in advance – logistics, plans and equipment decisions. This will leave your mind clear and free to concentrate on riding and training
- Don't worry about things beyond your control or influence – focus on what you can achieve on the day
- Visualize a successful outcome, and imagine yourself completing the event in good shape
- Stay positive – be optimistic about what lies ahead and your ability to tackle it
- View setbacks as temporary, and accept help if it's offered
- Feel good about yourself, your bike, your equipment – you have the best package you can have, and it will perform for you
- Commit yourself to completion – keep the end goal in mind, and don't contemplate giving up
- Adapt where you have to, but try to keep to the overall plan. Don't dwell on things that go wrong; deal with those you can, and move on
- Celebrate before you review – take some time to feel good about what you have achieved, and only then think about improvements for next time.

Under control and focussed on the task ahead.

CHAPTER 8

GETTING TO THE START LINE

Planning and Preparation

Dave Brailsford and British Cycling have received universal acclaim and acknowledgment for what they have achieved over the past few years, taking British track cycling to unprecedented levels of success, time and time again.

Whenever they are asked about their approach, the key members of Brailsford's team always refer to their attention to detail; they will say that if they can gain 1 per cent in a number of areas the total gain will make the difference between success and failure. They make sure that every aspect of the athlete's performance is reviewed and analysed in conjunction with rigorous attention to equipment, training, nutrition and preparation. Everything is thought through and meticulously planned, right down to the final moments before the event.

Why do they plan so carefully and precisely? There is an old saying which answers that question very neatly: 'To fail to prepare is to prepare to fail.'

The authors also believe in meticulous attention to detail and careful planning, even though we are amateur sportive riders and not élite international superstars. We still want to perform to our optimum capability, and we enjoy the process of bringing all the component parts together – it's all part of the experience. Experience has also taught us that taking care of the 'backroom' details early makes a big difference to the enjoyment and ultimate outcome of the event itself.

We plan early and we plan thoroughly to eliminate mishaps, stressful issues and crises, and this allows us to concentrate fully on the training programme we have mapped out. Knowing that transport, accommodation and equipment logistics are organized means that you can focus exclusively on the demands of the physical and mental preparation for the sportive.

Selecting a Suitable Event

Having decided to have a go at sportive riding, the next decision to be made is which event to enter. For the seasoned, cycling fit and experienced rider this may be about stepping up to face the toughest challenges available, and perhaps in exotic locations: the Étape du Tour, La Marmotte, the Maratona Dies Dolomites, Quebrantahuesos, Cape Argus Pick 'n' Pay, or the ultimate monster, Styrkeproven on the cold and windy roads of Norway. For the newcomer to

the world of sportives, the 25-miler starting from the local leisure centre may be the goal for the year, with the thought of progressing to the Shakespeare 100, the Silverstone Sportive or the Exmoor Beast the following season.

Which sportive to ride is an individual decision; it will be governed by your own aims and objectives, the influences around you, and your current state of fitness and experience. But once you have decided the broad parameters of the event you want to ride, then there are hundreds to choose from wherever you are located.

The decision to ride one or more sportives won't be taken lightly, and you will probably understand what you are letting yourself in for – long distances and tough climbing profiles, often climbing more than 3,000m in a 160km event. But no one can fully prepare themselves for some of these events – we still wonder exactly how we managed to complete Styrkeproven, all 540km of it, inside twenty hours, battling through never-ending cold, rain, wind and pain. This is an event that requires huge levels of focused training, high mileage, fitness, preparation, and above all, mental toughness.

For the newcomer to endurance cycling and sportives, there are hundreds of events to consider: from fast, fairly flat rides such as the Étape Caledonia in Scotland on closed roads, to long, hilly challenges such as the Fred Whitton Challenge in the Lake District or the Cornwall Tors in England. Nor do the hardest rides necessarily lie outside the UK: whilst the UK may not possess 30km climbs as found in the Alps or Pyrenees, it does contain plenty of tough, sharp climbs and varying weather conditions, which can combine to make some very tough challenges.

SPORTIVE REFERENCE POINTS

It is not our remit to fill the pages of this book with the names and details of sportives across the UK, Europe or the globe; others have done this far more comprehensively than we could. In our view the most comprehensive listing of sportives available to the UK rider is the online reference site dedicated to sportives, CycloSport (www.cyclosport.org); it is the best guide to events we know of, and we would recommend it as our preferred source of information. *Cycling Weekly* (www.cyclingweekly.co.uk) also publishes a good schedule, and a Google search of 'sportive' will deliver a comprehensive list of events.

Whichever event you choose, remember to make it appropriate to your level of fitness and ability to train and prepare.

A word of caution here: sportives such as the Étape du Tour have become very well publicised and even highly fashionable, and in recent years many people have entered but have then failed to train and plan for what is a very tough day in the saddle. All too often the Broom Wagon brings them in at the end, weary, disillusioned and disappointed – and maybe even lost to sportives for the future. As an aside, between about 2004 and 2007 the UK riders at Étape gained the worst reputation for under preparation of all the nations participating, a statistic that has happily been rectified since as riders have come to recognize the degree of preparation required.

Do some research, identify potential events, and understand the demands likely to be placed on you on the day. Understand the training, travel and other requirements and prepare properly. Try to get the balance right between distance, difficulty, location, length, amount of climbing, number of entrants, likely weather conditions, logistics of travel, accommodation and cost. Remember, you don't have to travel far if you live in the UK, France, Spain and most European countries, to find a number of events available to you. For us, living in central UK, for example, there are probably at least fifty sportives to choose from each season within 80km of our homes.

The Preparation Plan

The sooner you fix the challenge in your mind the better, and the earlier you commit yourself and start preparing, the more likely you are to be ready and fit for it. So highlight the date of the key event in your calendar, or even better, buy a training calendar and put together a programme that fits the time available and which schedules the training hours and miles required.

If one of your goals is to shed a few unwanted kilos – as it will be for most of us – then make sure you pick an event that allows you to plan a gradual, steady weight loss programme rather than having to go on a crash diet that isn't sustainable, which can cause serious negative consequences for your general health. As Bradley Wiggins demonstrated for the 2009 Tour de France by shedding around 6kg from his élite athlete's physique, it is possible even for toned athletes to slim down and achieve maximum power-to-weight performance, but only over many months and in a carefully controlled and planned regime.

We would recommend that the preparation plan sets out the overall targets and breaks the time period leading up to the event into shorter periods, such as weekly or ten-day training cycles. Set clear and measurable goals throughout the schedule, and make these realistic so that they fit into the overall context of your home, work and general life demands and pressures.

It may also help to have a parallel plan, where you map out the various organizational and administrative tasks necessary to make the event happen smoothly, such as travel arrangements, accommodation, bike maintenance and so on. From personal experience, if travelling abroad by plane to a sportive, book the seats – and the bike box – as early as possible; we once had a situation where we could get ourselves back from the event, but there was no room for the bikes on the plane, as often the airlines have a maximum number of bike boxes they will put on a flight. For the most popular UK events such as Étape Caledonia or The Dragon Ride, organize accommodation as early as possible, as it goes very quickly once the entries fill up, and you definitely don't want to be located an hour away from the start if you don't have to be.

Once the plan is written, pin it up in a place where it is easily visible, keep it updated, and modify it as events dictate. Life has a habit of getting in the way of the best laid plans, so without compromising the overall goals, you might have to modify and adapt the plan to suit circumstances. Specifically, don't try to 'chase' lost training miles unless a clear window of opportunity opens up. Just accept that a training session has gone, and move on to the next one. If you increase mileage too suddenly, or try to catch up on missed outings, the risk of over-training and injury increases. The golden rule is not to increase mileage by more than 10 per cent week on week, and in fact building up on a monthly basis, if the schedule allows, is safer and more sustainable.

Let family, friends and workmates know what you are doing – let them see the plan, even – because there's nothing like a family member or a work-mate or peer pressure to keep you focused through the long, dark winter training months. If you are entering an event with others, then share your plans and your actual results.

Get together every month if possible if you plan to ride the event in a group, particularly if you don't live in close proximity or ride together, and arrange what we call 'benchmark rides' to assess where you are against the schedule. There's nothing like the pressure of meeting up and riding with the group to keep the focus on the training programme. In addition, and to provide a focus for the winter, we always plan a week's training camp in Spain in February, and none of us would dream of turning up in Denia, Costa Blanca, at our training base (www.TrainInSpain.net) having let the winter mileage slip too far behind.

Although we realize that a few days in the sun isn't possible for everyone, we would strongly encourage those who intend to make sportive riding the basis of their cycling year to consider joining a group somewhere. During the bleak winter months it creates a focal point to aim for, and once on the camp, the warm weather mileage definitely adds some groundwork to the overall training plan. The camaraderie and opportunity to ride with a few like-minded people is great as well.

Pack your bike box or bag early and avoid rushing the job.

spares. Another word of caution here: as you pack the bike and the gear in the final stages before leaving home, it may not be a good idea to let anyone 'help you pack'....

We arrived in Toulouse for the 2007 Étape du Tour to discover a distinct lack of pedals and chains, helpfully 'packed' back in the cupboard by a darling two-year-old daughter, and now 1,000 miles away in England. Our Étape preparation had not included walking 8km through a busy French city to locate a decent bike shop that sold compatible pedals....

Checklists will help you ensure that everything comes together for the event. If you build your own checklists, then just make sure that you cover the following:

- Event and logistics information/paperwork (including passports and tickets)
- Bike and associated equipment (pump, spares etc.)
- Clothing
- Food and fluids.

Then make sure you know what you are going to carry and where, and if you are travelling by plane, how you are going to split things between bike box or bag, and holdall or hand luggage. Some airlines are now imposing what seem to be ridiculously low weight and size restrictions, and hefty surcharges if you get it wrong. There is nothing more stressful and aggravating than having to open up and repack boxes, bags and luggage under pressure with a 50m queue of irritable holidaymakers watching you and blaming you for the delay.

Practical Arrangements

Many of the popular events sell out literally within hours of entries opening, so make sure you know when you can enter. Book the flights, train tickets or coach seats early as well; not only will you be able to file these time-consuming details away and not have to worry about them, but you will probably save money too. Check that hotels, guest houses or bed and breakfast establishments are 'bike friendly' and situated close to the start/finish area. It makes a big difference to be able to build the bike and check your gear in a hassle-free spot, and to be able to spin down to the start or get to the car parking area quickly and easily on the morning of the sportive. Many of us are very protective of our bikes, so check that the hotel will allow the machine to be wheeled into the room or safely stored in a locked storeroom.

Checklists

When travelling to an event, use a checklist of equipment and nutritional items to be taken with you and to be carried on the bike during the sportive; we have included some recommendations in the book, but each individual has different needs and slightly different strategies for food, clothing and

Losses and Insurance

Pack everything several days ahead of departure; make sure everything fits as you plan it to, and if possible, weigh your bike box and bags, just to make sure you are under the limits. If travelling with a heavy bike box or bag, you will probably have to check in a bag, and it may make sense to split items up so that if one bag is lost, you have a fighting chance of arriving with enough gear to ride in, even if temporarily.

In practice and reality, if the airline loses an item of your equipment such as the bike box, unless they will give a definite assurance that it has been located and is being sent on a specific flight, then we recommend that you immediately set about making contingency plans rather than hoping it will turn up. Head straight to the nearest/best bike shop in town and see if they have suitable machines to rent. Speak to the organizers and see if they can help, and don't spend all the available time worrying, hoping and cursing the airline. Make the best of things and decide whether or not you can ride the event. Then refocus on your final, amended preparations and channel your frustration towards the culprits into a successful ride.

Afterwards chase as hard as you can for the return of the item and/or for compensation. But note well that the small print of most airline terms and conditions limits the claim in the event of loss to a fraction of the true cost of your possessions, particularly if a bike box has vanished. So we would recommend having secondary insurance from your own household insurance company, the CTC or British Cycling to cover the real cost of replacement. Take it from us, the outlay is absolutely worth it, especially if it includes accident and medical cover. We have both lost equipment, had equipment smashed, and crashed and been hospitalized. This sort of thing can happen when you compete frequently.

Pre-Event Preparations

Pre-Event Tapering

It is beyond the capability of even the strongest rider to train and compete intensively non-stop throughout an extended period without a break: rest and recovery must play a part in the overall plan. When focusing on a specific event most athletes achieve their best performances when they ease back and modify the training effort over a short period ahead of the actual event or competition. This is called 'tapering', and it is as appropriate to the amateur as it is to the élite cyclist. The fitter the individual, the shorter the taper, but there are some guidelines we would recommend.

First of all, you should try to achieve your maximum level of training workload and intensity about two weeks ahead of the event date, and reduce the workload down to around 25 per cent of peak during the week before the event. This is known as peaking, and is especially relevant if you are aiming at a single event in a season. The base fitness you have achieved throughout the winter will have been augmented by power training and specific sessions, and your body will be ready to deliver.

The key stages in the taper are as follows:

Reduction of training time and mileage: Begin to reduce your weekly totals two weeks away from the event date so that your volume is about 25 per cent of normal during the week before the sportive. Remember, it is actually beneficial to continue training before the event, and still at fairly high intensity, but the duration of the sessions should be reduced.

Engage in specific work: Base your final activity on the event on which you are focused; so if it is a flattish profile, work on faster, bigger gear sessions to simulate the effort required for the event.

Maintain the intensity of your workouts: Make them shorter than during the previous training period. Most current research indicates that your body recovers faster from short, high intensity sessions in the imminent lead-up to an event.

Begin to focus your mind on the event itself: Practise the visualization techniques already discussed. If you have to travel to the sportive the day before, then go for a light, short spin once you have built the bike in order to remove lactic acid and get your legs turning again after the journey – but resist the temptation to ride too far, too hard.

Pre-Event Bike Check

The day before you set off for the event, if local, or before you pack your bike box for a longer journey, do a final pre-event check – you will be depending on this piece of machinery for your success, and you have to be confident that as far as you can ascertain, it won't let you down at a crucial moment. The check should include the following:

- **Frame:** Check that there are no cracks, particularly at the key stress points such as tube joints and head and bottom bracket areas
- **Brakes:** Make sure the brake pads have enough 'tread' on them; many now have wear indicators to help you. Ensure that the pads touch the rims at the same time; off-centre braking can be dangerous, and it pushes the wheel off line, creating instability
- **Tyres:** Let about half the air out and then inspect the tyre, starting and finishing at the valve, for any cuts, wear or tears. Pinch the tyre as you revolve it so that you can feel any sharp stones or other items, and pull them out. Most tyres will have a few minor cuts, although we would recommend that at least for the main event of your season you should fit a new set the week before. When you fit tyres, think about the likely surface conditions; if there is rain forecast, you are likely to encounter gravel and other debris washed on to the road, so a pair of reinforced tyres will be advisable
- **Tyre pressures:** Should not be set too high (*see also* pp. 26–27, section on equipment); to some extent it is a question of personal choice, but will change depending on rider weight and conditions on the day. We recommend 100 to 120psi as the optimal range between comfort and rolling resistance. A lower pressure may be advisable in warm weather when the heat of the road and braking can cause the air to expand, which will frequently lead to a puncture if the pressures are too high to start with, or also when roads are wet and additional grip through increased tyre/road contact is advisable. Inflate your tyres the night before the event as we have experienced punctures and valves snapping when pumping tyres just before you move to the start line – not an ideal, stress-free start to your sportive
- **Cables:** Look for splits or other damage, and make sure cables run freely and are not trapped or pinched
- **Bolts:** Check handlebars, stem, seat post, saddle, pedals and any other allen nuts or bolts which may have been loosened during disassembly. Do not over-tighten bolts,

especially on carbon bars and seat posts. It is worth investing in a torque key, which will tension the bolt to exactly the right pressure

- **Wheels:** Check all the spokes for possible damage, that the wheels spin 'true', and that the hubs are rotating smoothly and easily. Check for cracks or dents in the rims
- **Headset:** Shouldn't move when the front brake is applied and the bike is pushed forwards. It shouldn't stick to the right or left when the front of the bike is off the ground and the bars are rolled to each side, and there shouldn't be any rattling or other noises from the headset area. If any of the above exists, then loosen the headset bolt, loosen the stem bolts and then re-seat the headset. Tighten the headset bolt, tighten the stem bolts and then slightly release the headset bolt again
- **Gears/flywheels:** Should be clean and free from dirt or other obstruction which might prevent smooth operation. It is common for riders to forget to clean the flywheels in the derailleurs, and this will cause the gears to jump – not desirable on a 20 per cent incline on a damp morning, and at the very least irritating and energy sapping over a 100-mile event. Lubricate key pivot points on derailleurs, flywheels and brakes
- **Chain:** Check for wear with a chain tool if you have one, or at least check the tension and the links as the cranks turn. Beware and note well: the chain is probably the least checked, maintained and changed component on many bikes, and is perhaps the most crucial
- **Bike computer:** Check that the speed pick-up is close enough to the magnet and that there is a reading. If your feeding strategy or pacing is dependent on distance then it can be very frustrating to roll out of the start only to realize that your speed and distance are not being picked up
- **Saddle and seat post:** Make sure bolts are secure and tightened, and that the saddle is horizontal and securely fixed to the seat post
- **Apply lubricant:** To chain, gears and brakes, but wipe off the excess. Remember, a clean bike feels better, looks better, and will definitely function better
- Last, and usually forgotten: **inspect the cleat bolts in your shoes**; no one remembers, but a loose cleat and a lost bolt can end your hopes of a fast time as surely as any other mechanical problem.

On Arrival

If you are travelling far and arrive the day before, on arrival check in to your accommodation and focus on building the bike back up as soon as possible. This allows you to check things at the earliest opportunity and have maximum time to deal with any loss or damage that may have happened in transit.

Once back together again, take the bike out for a light ride, partly to check it over and partly to help work the journey out of your legs. As we said earlier, never think that damage will never happen to you: we have experienced several incidents, and have had to make very hasty alternative repair plans too soon before the start of a major event for comfort.

If you are arriving on the morning of the event, try to leave enough time for a last-minute equipment check; it is amazing how even after the shortest of journeys to an event, something changes once the bike is rebuilt – a brake jams, a bolt has loosened or a puncture mysteriously appears.

Use the checklist in Appendix II to make sure you have the right clothes, spares, food, fluids, gels and other items, and that they all fit where you planned them to fit about the bike and your person. This last-minute preparation of packing your jersey, donning jacket and gloves and so on, always takes longer than you think, so make time for it in your plan.

Try not to make unforced last-minute changes, and stick to your pre-event plan unless something unavoidable forces a change on you. If that happens, try to keep changes to a minimum. Your tried and tested equipment and routines are always better when the event is ahead of you.

A Word On Registration

Like every other aspect of preparation and planning, register as early as possible. If the organizers and your travel plans allow, then register the day before the sportive. If that isn't possible, then leave as much time as possible for this process in the morning of the event. It often involves queuing, and some organizers are better at the process than others. The more time you leave yourself, the better.

Registration can be fun, but it often leads to a build-up of nervous tension, and that in turn wastes energy, so get in there, register, and get out again.

Once registered, go through the ritual of pinning or sticking event numbers on, and securing timing chips if available, carefully and methodically. If a wheel has been loosened to fit a timing chip, then go back over the wheel and brake alignment checks once the chip has been secured. Don't rush these tasks, as that will just lead to more nerves and stress, and possibly cause some damage.

Sleep/Rest

We have talked a lot about the bike and about planning, but now a few words on sleep, rest and recovery. Recovery is the least discussed aspect of any training plan, but it matters as much as the hours of physical effort put into training. The night before the event might not bring a lot of sleep for most people: nerves and adrenalin will probably keep you awake. The good news is that at least for one night or so, research has shown that a lack of actual sleep does not materially affect performance during the event: it is rest which is crucial. So remember the old cycling adage: 'Never stand when you can sit, and never sit when you can lie down.'

SLEEP, THE CRUCIAL INGREDIENT

Very few training manuals talk much about sleep as a component part of the training and preparation programme, other than making the basic observation that you need a decent night's rest before the event itself. But sleep in a long-term context is a crucial element in preparation for any strenuous activity. If you are to maximize your physical potential, then the periods in which you do nothing and rest are as crucial as those in which you are training hard.

It is during rest and sleep periods that the body – and the mind – recover and regenerate, and it is only at these times that 'adaptation', as it is called, takes place, when the body builds more capability to deal with the training loads being placed upon it. Every athlete needs a productive sleep period, comprising enough hours of rest/sleep and a natural wake time. Sleep periods will ideally be made up of ninety-minute cycles, and alternate between light and deep sleep patterns. Now of course you can't actually directly control these cycles yourself, but you can at least create an environment in which the right patterns are promoted. Sleeping patterns change with age, and external factors such as stress, anxiety and work pressures contribute to poor sleeping habits. External factors, including noise, light and temperature, all make a difference as well, and the timing of evening meals and drinks can affect the body's ability to establish the right patterns.

Ideally, we need around eight hours' sleep every night to allow for rest and recovery, and in order to gain maximum benefit from the sleep period you need to work backwards from your own natural wake-up point to allow for enough ninety-minute sleep cycles to occur. Most healthy adults will need four or five sleep cycles to achieve the best results, so work backwards from your natural or necessary wake time to define what time to go to bed.

The tendency for most people is to go to sleep too late, having eaten too late, and to wake too often for visits to the bathroom. Maintaining a well balanced diet with regular and measured food and fluid intakes promotes healthy sleep patterns, and the last meal should be taken no later than three hours before sleep. Try to avoid sleeping when hungry or with a full bladder, and if a snack is needed, then make it something easily digestible and light.

Maintain your bedroom temperature at about 16°C to 18°C, use ambient, natural light, and start the sleep session if possible on your 'weaker' side – thus a right-handed person would sleep on their left side, at least to begin with. Experiment with pillow heights and positions to establish the correct posture for your specific physique: the ideal is to achieve a position where your body and head are more or less supported by the mattress, as if a pillow isn't necessary; then apply a pillow, which simply provides a little more support and comfort.

Most of us tend to ignore sleep when we consider our plans and programme; this is a mistake, as much of the benefit from training can be dissipated by not getting the right amount and type of sleep and rest.

Immediately before the event, get as much rest as possible, and don't waste valuable reserves of carbohydrate and other fuels. Although the event may be accompanied by many ancillary events, try to minimize the time you spend walking around and participating the night before; we know that sounds rather boring, but it's up to you – are you interested in riding to your potential after hundreds of hours of training, or compromising your performance by using up valuable energy on a few minutes entertainment?

Pre-Event Nutrition

We have discussed carbo-loading as part of the build-up to the sportive itself, but on the day of the event it is essential to take on board the right fuel for the task ahead. No matter how much you consume before you start you will still need to eat and drink during the race, but a balanced and appropriate pre-event meal will help you perform to your optimum.

It is important to leave enough time between the pre-event meal and when the exertion starts, so we would recommend breakfast about three hours before start time. That may mean an early wake-up call, but your food needs to digest before you get on the bike.

Eat a breakfast made up of complex carbohydrates such as porridge, muesli, cereal or toasted wholewheat bread, accompanied by bananas or other fruits. Use skimmed milk where available. Pro riders will often consume pasta or rice, too, but that may be a bit too much for the sportive rider at 05:00 on a chilly morning. Take on board some protein as well: a couple of eggs or a light mushroom omelette would be ideal. You can also start the caffeine intake with a cup or two of tea or coffee.

Stay hydrated: we usually sip regularly from a bottle of low strength carbohydrate drink, from waking right up to getting to the start.

About thirty or forty minutes before the start eat a banana or a few dried fruits such as figs or apricots, or perhaps an energy bar, and take another drink of sports drink, or coffee if you prefer. We would then recommend that you consume an energy gel immediately before the sportive starts to give you an early boost over the first, often frantic, miles.

What To Take On the Ride

When it comes to decisions about what to carry during the sportive itself, the balance lies somewhere between the practicality (and weight, of course) of what you can stuff into various jersey pockets and seat packs, and what is provided by the organizers and available during the ride.

There is no point in carrying unnecessary food, tools and clutter – but it is essential to be able to mend a puncture, tighten a bolt and take in enough fluid and food to be able to cope with most minor situations away from support

Basic nutritional elements for a long sportive.

vehicles or feed stations. It is important to gather these items before you travel to the event – do not rely upon purchasing items at or before the event.

The night before the sportive make sure you lay out all your kit, fill your bottles and pack your jersey pocket as a final check that you have everything you need.

Every rider will make their own specific decisions as to what to take on a ride, but our recommendations for the start of a typical 100-mile sportive with two feed stations built into the route are outlined below.

Event Nutrition

- Three or four gel sachets with caffeine supplement to be used at 25, 50, 65 and 90 miles
- Two or three energy bars to be eaten slowly and regularly during the event either side of feed stations
- A handful of dried fruit and a banana to augment and add some variety to the energy bars
- A sachet or two of energy drink powder to be used when replenishing water bottles (it's not a great idea to take on a new and different formula at feed stations; this can lead to stomach problems during the event).

This load fits into your jersey pockets, and of course gets progressively smaller and lighter as the event progresses.

We use feed stations principally to take on water, and only consume simple foods such as a banana or maybe a currant bun or piece of cake if offered before setting off again. In our earlier riding days we made the same mistake as many: we saw the feed stations as an opportunity to stop, chat and rest – and later realized that our total elapsed time for the event had been significantly lengthened by our socializing at the feed stations. Of course, not every sportive rider is bothered about their total time, and the feed stations then do provide the opportunity to recover and regroup before the next stage of the ride.

Clothing

We recommend always having a lightweight rainproof jacket or gilet tucked into a pocket even if the weather is very warm. Conditions can and do change dramatically during a six- or ten-hour event, and even on a hot day a long descent can be very cold after a demanding climb. Do not rely on just a wind-proof jacket: if in doubt buy a lightweight jacket that is also rain-proof or at least shower-proof. If arm

A seat pack holds absolute essentials.

or knee warmers are necessary at the start, then these also tuck away into a pocket after removal.

Other Equipment

A mobile phone could make the difference between getting help quickly and continuing, or abandoning an event entirely; useful in emergencies, it doesn't take up much space and doesn't add too much weight. If you are riding with a group, then just make sure there are a couple of mobiles between you. It is always sensible to carry some cash; we have rarely used it, but a £10 note in the seat pack (where it won't get soggy from sweat) covers most emergencies.

If you are following a non-signed route, then you may well need a small plastic bag to hold the directions, as these will also very quickly cease to be legible if carried in a back pocket with no protection. If you wear protective glasses (and we would never ride without them) with interchangeable lenses, then the second set will be tucked away somewhere as well.

Saddle Bag

Most sportive riders will use a small bag or seat pack located under the saddle and attached to the saddle rails and seat post; it is also an option on longer rides to fix a small strap-fixed bag on the top tube, as triathletes often do. These are neat, light and easy to access. If you use one, then this is where to keep the gels and energy bars which need to be reached frequently and with minimum fuss. Our recommendation is to place food and gels into your jersey pockets and stick to a small seat pack with a number of essential items:

- Tyre levers × 2
- Spare inner tube
- Self-adhesive patches × 2
- Mini pump (if not fixed to the frame next to the bottle cage, or in your rear pocket)
- £10 or €10 note
- Mini tool or set of allen keys.

This load will fit into most small bags, and will allow you to deal with a range of minor mishaps and get back on the road to complete the event. The reality is that if something more serious breaks or goes wrong, the likelihood is that your event is over, and you will need to wait for the Broom Wagon or support vehicle to get help.

Do check your seat pack before an event – it is too easy to use items such as inner tubes and patches in an event, and not refill the bag with replacements. If you have been lucky for a while and haven't used the spare tube, then check it is still all right, or replace it with a new one before a major event. There is no point in spoiling a good time by finding out that the perished old tube in the seat bag is no use to you at precisely the moment you need it most.

A small detail, perhaps, but we always use long-valved inner tubes even with standard rim wheels: fumbling about trying to get enough valve to poke out of a flat tyre in order to get a decent clamp with a small pump is simply a waste of time; use a long valve tube and the process is quicker and more efficient.

Warming Up

Here we are going to settle for pragmatism and practical reality above 'best practice'. The chances are that your event will have an early morning start time and you may well have arrived slightly late, queued for registration and had trouble fixing on your race number, so you are unlikely to go through a proper warm-up routine as the pro rider does before a Tour de France stage. Equally your performance will be improved, and injury will be less likely, if you do manage some warm-up before the start, for the following reasons:

- Muscles function better when warm because they contract with greater force and release faster, giving a more powerful action. So increasing muscle temperature is beneficial
- As the muscles begin to operate, they require increased blood flow, and the blood vessels need to dilate to deliver this
- As the human body exercises, a series of chemical/hormonal changes occurs in order to assist the body/engine to perform to its optimum. These changes start quickly, but take a while to come into full operation, so warming up allows this process to start
- The warm-up process gives the competitor the chance finally to focus on the event ahead, and clear their mind of unnecessary clutter.

For a warm-up to be useful, you need to achieve a reasonably high level of effort whilst warming up, so we would recommend taking a short spin for a few minutes on a fairly level surface, before finding a short climb and raising your heart rate and lung function. Otherwise, do a few sprints after a few minutes of riding steadily. We recommend combining these warm-ups with the stretches suitable for warm-up sessions discussed earlier (see pp. 64–73, section on stretching). Don't overdo things, and get to the line warm but fresh; the advantage will be felt in an event where a sharp climb comes early on in the ride.

Final Moments Before Starting

Confident in the knowledge that you have prepared to the best of your ability, you are ready to go. You've relaxed and had an early night – although sleep is the best preparation before the event, as long as you get sufficient rest your body won't be seriously affected in the very short term, and you should be able to deliver a good performance on the day.

If you have travelled to the sportive on the day of the event itself, then follow much of the same procedure as we have covered for arrival the day before. After arriving at the venue for the event, build your bike as necessary (hopefully this would just mean re-fitting front and rear wheels after transit from your home or accommodation), do some light stretching and warm-up, breathe deeply, focus your mind, and make your way – not too early, but in plenty of time – to the start line.

Do not waste energy in pushing to the front or worrying how far back you are – the event will give you plenty of time to catch and pass people, and you will be riding to your own strategy anyway. Many riders fret far too much about their start position; the reality is that unless you are an élite rider going for the podium, over the course of six, seven or ten hours you will have ample opportunity and time to make up a couple of minutes lost by starting from a later pen. The energy lost in stressing about this just isn't worth it.

Experience Says …

- Plan, enter and make arrangements early – you can then focus on controlling your physical and mental preparation for the event
- Create a training and nutrition programme that allows you to peak for the event
- Balance your training with work and family life; you need support from those around you
- Set sensible and measurable goals, specific to the event you are aiming at
- Pack several days ahead of the event or departure. Use checklists for bike, gear, clothes, food, fluids and logistics
- On arrival, build the bike and check your kit as soon as possible to allow for the discovery of any breakages or forgotten items to be replaced
- Register early if you can't the night before, and get the logistics out of the way
- Go for a gentle ride to check out bike and body
- Lay out your kit the night before, and do a final check that you have everything
- Take your time over the final preparations – make this part of your build-up
- Get an early night, but don't worry too much if you can't sleep – rest is more important than sleep for a single night
- Don't fret about your start position – a few places won't make any difference over a long event
- Relax, focus and visualize success – don't waste energy worrying.

CHAPTER 9

RIDING THE EVENT

At the Start

You are in the start area and surrounded by tens, hundreds, or maybe thousands of fellow riders. Each of you will be feeling nervous, apprehensive, excited, tired, impatient – and above all, raring to go.

It is important not to waste too much nervous energy before the start of the event, and in this regard during the 2007 Étape du Tour from Foix to Loudenvielle (196km) we learnt a valuable lesson. When you enter the Étape you are eventually allocated a start number of anywhere between numbers 500 to 7,500 or 8,000 (the first few hundred starters are allocated to VIPs or sponsor invites). Riders start in 'pens' of 500 or so, depending on the start number. Our numbers, when they came through, were in the 5,500s, and we immediately became preoccupied with the fact that we were nearer the last starter than the first; before a pedal had even turned our thoughts were on the Broom Wagon's proximity, sweeping up the slow riders.

With two weeks to go before the event, part of our attention switched to making sure we got to the front of that pen (moving from 5,500 to 5,000), to make up ground. The morning of the event arrived, and we rushed to the coach, rushed off it, and rushed to the pen – and over a 185km event and nine hours of riding it was all a complete waste of effort, as there was plenty of time to pick up speed and momentum, and catch those who had charged off recklessly.

So by all means try to ensure you stay with any riding partners you may have, but accept your place and enjoy the atmosphere – and remember that every rider, irrespective of ability or experience, will be feeling like you.

Stay Warm

One of the characteristics of a sportive is that it often starts at 7 or 8 o'clock in the morning. This generally means that the temperature at the start of the event will be very different to what you will experience in the late morning/early afternoon, and usually equates to getting cold as you go to, and wait for, the start. It is therefore always a good idea to wear a lightweight waterproof jacket or gilet. If we need protection we wear a jacket, as the long sleeves save the need to wear arm warmers which, when the temperature rises, need to be removed and then take up one of the rear pockets on your jersey. The lightweight jacket

The start of the Étape Caledonia, Scotland.

can also be put on at the top of climbs to protect you against the cold; this is especially valuable on long European descents.

Another part of your body that warrants special attention early into any ride is your hands. Cold hands early in a ride is the bane of many a cyclist, and we tackle this problem by wearing a pair of surgical-type gloves underneath our cycling gloves. These give protection from some of the wind chill, and they can be easily disposed of at the first feed station if the temperature has risen sufficiently.

The Early Miles

You will be shuffling forwards as your turn comes to cross the line, so be sure you have one foot clipped into the pedals because as you roll over the start line your timing chip will trigger a beep and your time will start.

In the first phase of any ride there are certain crucial areas to focus on: you should be aware of other riders; ride for yourself, avoiding starting too fast; and conserve energy.

The first miles often feel tough as the pace is high and your body hasn't fully warmed up. Don't worry; settle into your rhythm and remember – everyone else feels the same.

Be Aware of Other Riders

While you may be the most talented bike rider in the world, we can assure you that many of your co-participants may not be as skilled, and in the excitement of the start and the scramble for position it is very easy to knock a wheel or elbow and be taken down. Be very vigilant at the start of a big ride: look for gaps, and maintain as much distance and separation from other riders as the circumstances allow.

Ride For Yourself

Often you may be riding with friends, and the camaraderie of riding an event together is a great experience. However, after the start, especially in the larger European events, you may be split from your riding partners – but don't worry about this, or spend energy trying to get back together. If this happens it is better to have a pre-agreed time into the ride to pause and let the lead rider wait and regroup the team; this way you can focus on staying out of trouble and maintaining your own pace.

Nowadays when we ride we simply agree to meet up if circumstances permit, but essentially we ride individually, as we are all different and during the event we will all have strengths and weaknesses, slow points and periods of energy. There is probably no point in trying to stay together with friends unless your riding abilities are very similar. One of the great attractions of a sportive is that you are amongst riders of all abilities, and you regularly make new friends as you ride together.

Don't Start Too Fast

One of the most tempting things to do early in an event is to go too hard, too early. As groups form it is common to find yourself riding at above your heart-rate threshold. In a Gran Fondo in Italy or in the Étape du Tour in France you will find that the locals will set off at top speed and as groups form it is common to find yourself riding at your limit very early in the event. Our experience tells us to back off and maintain a heart rate which is within your comfort zone – there are always riders or groups on the road that will be at your pace, so maintain a comfortable level of effort and ride yourself into a rhythm that you can maintain.

During your training and preparation you should have worked out what your own specific 'threshold' is: that is to say, the effort level which keeps you just inside aerobic limits and therefore burning the right fuels and maximizing endurance capability. You can monitor this by your heart rate, and it is important to stay within threshold as much as possible, no matter what is going on around you.

Sometimes if you are feeling strong and find yourself on the front of a group, it is tempting to lead out too often or find yourself riding off the front of the group. We can tell you from experience that this is wasted effort which burns energy and which can lead to burn-out later in the event. Just as in a professional race a breakaway group will rarely stay away, the same applies in a sportive. The fact is that a group of riders, even working relatively inefficiently, will be faster than an individual. If you find yourself off the front, then check your pace and allow the group to catch you. After a period of time you will reach other groups or will find three or four riders within the group who are clearly stronger. If this happens, ask if they want to work as a smaller group, and by working together you will start to move away from the other riders who do not have the strength to stay with you.

The secret of achieving your best time in a sportive lies not just in your own fitness and mental state, but in your ability to work with others and to identify groups that will pull you along faster.

Conserve Energy

As you ride further into the event your legs will loosen and your breathing should settle into a rhythm. It is time to look for opportunities to conserve energy. This will mean riding 'smart' in terms of sharing the workload with fellow riders. If you find yourself leading the group or riding partners too often, do not be afraid of signalling for them to come through to the front (flick your elbow outwards to tell them to come through), and make your way back down the line as other riders come through. You would typically expect to spend no longer than one or two minutes on the front of a group in any one turn.

If a rider who has attached himself to your group fails to take a turn at the front, then do not be afraid to make your views known; we have had to be very 'blunt' on a few occasions with 'wheel suckers' who try to get a free ride.

The Middle Section

Work Together

If you find yourself with a group of riders whom you don't know, then ask other riders if they want to work together.

We have already covered the fundamentals of riding in a group (see p. 81, section on technique) as this can be a very rewarding experience if you are aware of the etiquette and 'rules of the road'. Furthermore in terms of sportive performance, riding in a group can have huge benefits if you make wise choices about when and who to ride with. The advantages are not only confined to increased pace and energy conservation, but also motivation and feeling part of a 'team'. Many of our best performances have been through planned group riding – for example, in the 300km Vatternrundan sportive in Sweden where we ride as a team of eight or ten riders, sharing the workload and riding to a disciplined code, led by a nominated leader. We even have a protocol whereby the whole team slows down every hour, just for three minutes, to allow for calls of nature. Thus the rider who has answered the call of nature doesn't have to time trial back to the group as it speeds away up the road.

If you can get a group working together, then it is important that a rider coming to the front maintains a steady pace so as not to create a gap with the second rider. As you come off the front, look over your shoulder; let the group come through, and the last rider should tell you 'Last man'. You then know you can pull in and assume your position in the train. Use this time to recover, take a drink and let your fellow riders take the wind. You will be amazed at how much fresher and stronger you will feel at the end of a sportive where you have been able to work cleverly with a group of like-minded individuals.

Eat and Drink Often

It is important to feed and hydrate your body sufficiently to provide energy at a consistent level through the ride. This means eating and drinking a little but often, and to start doing so from early in the ride. It also means eating before you feel hungry, and certainly means stopping at most, if not all of the allocated feed stations. Missing food stations and the opportunity to eat and fill your water bottles is a major factor in poor performance later in an event.

During a typical sportive lasting between five to ten hours a competitor will burn anything up to 5,000, 7,000 or even more calories. A highly trained athlete can store no more than about 2,000 to 2,500 calories in immediately available fuel such as carbohydrates and muscle glycogens, which is what you should use for sudden increases in tempo or hard, short efforts. So you simply have to train your body to use fat as its main fuel. With training, fat becomes the primary endurance fuel, and you probably have around 100,000 calories of energy available from that source, which is plenty for any sportive; but nonetheless, if the rider doesn't replenish carbohydrate stores as they are also used, the likelihood is that he or she will encounter the dreaded 'bonk'.

A good strategy is to start to snack on a high carbohydrate energy bar within about forty-five minutes to one hour of the event start, and we would consume an energy gel at regular intervals as well. As we said earlier, snip the top off the energy bars with a pair of scissors before you ride – this makes the bar instantly accessible, and you don't have to tug, chew and gnaw to get the top opened as you ride along.

Remember also that you need to replace up to a litre of fluid an hour when riding hard, so try to drink every ten minutes or so once into the main body of the event. A dehydration-induced bodyweight loss of 5 per cent can lead to a reduction in performance of 20 per cent or greater, so keep drinking.

Consume a few dried apricots or figs if you can eat them to vary the diet during the ride, and try to eat on flat or even gentle downhill stretches, as this will minimize the impact of chewing and swallowing on your breathing pattern. Somehow, however, it always seems that every time you take a mouthful of energy bar, you turn a corner and see a long hill looming ahead of you….

Finally, try to keep a gel sachet for the last section of the event, to give you an immediate boost and the ability to push hard for the finish.

Don't Hang Around

Whilst we know it is critical to stop at food stations to replenish your supplies, set yourself a limit of five minutes, and enter with a purpose. Priority one is to fill your water bottles. Priority two is to collect food: work on the 'eat one, pocket one' principle, so munch a banana whilst you are in the feed station and put one in your pocket to eat while you ride.

Your third priority is to use the toilet facilities if available and required. Be prepared in the bigger events to encounter a bit of a scrum, and if you can hold out comfortably, then wait for the second or later stops to relieve the call of nature. Agree with your riding mates that one of you will get food and drink while another holds the bikes. Stick together so as not to lose time searching for wandering riding partners.

As we have said above, energy bars and gels should be taken at regular intervals – do not leave them all for the final third of the event. Over a 100-mile sportive we recommend taking gels at 25, 50, 65 and 90 miles. Spreading the time between gels and taking a drink after each will help you maintain a more consistent level of energy. Gels containing caffeine can really provide a noticeable boost to the way you feel and also promote fat-burning.

We recommend having enough gel/bars to last the whole ride, rather than taking bars from the feed stops; your choice of gel/bars is very personal, and it is common for energy foods you are unfamiliar with to cause stomach problems later in the ride when you are struggling to digest anything. Most gels deliver a boost once absorbed by the system; we find it useful to try to time the consumption of a gel with arrival at the foot of a long climb or tough section.

Hydrate Properly

It is tempting, especially in your first sportives, to err on the side of caution by drinking litres and litres of fluids and to over-hydrate before and during an event. Now this is not such a bad thing, but it can mean numerous forced 'rest stops', which will lose you time. If you are drinking a small amount but often, this can be controlled, and as you become more experienced you will learn the optimal amount of fluid to take, when taking into account weather conditions, effort and distance. In our experience you can match your fluid intake to that processed by your body and lost through sweat. This will mean fewer 'rest stops' and a faster time. However, a common cause of underperformance in sportives is to fail to drink enough, causing cramps, so it is important that you balance the need to take on board enough energy and electrolyte drinks in relation to the conditions and how you feel on the day.

It is worth testing how much sweat you lose as part of your training by weighing yourself before and after a ride to see how much weight you lose. This will give you a fair indication of how much fluid you as an individual need to take in during a given event. Fluid intake varies enormously from person to person, so don't just follow the advice of your mates, or slavishly adhere to guidelines in a training book, but try to work out as you ride and train what suits your own specific requirements. Don't, however, under-hydrate at any stage, so err on the side of drinking too much, rather than too little.

We suggest you take two sachets of your chosen energy drink to refill your bottles, and also a couple of electrolyte tablets that will dissolve quickly into your drink and replace lost minerals such as potassium, calcium and magnesium, all of which are essential for the muscle system to function correctly.

The Final Push

Hopefully, you will have ridden well and without problems for two thirds of the event distance, and you will probably be approaching the final feed stop. This is a crucial period in the ride. If you have eaten well, maintained hydration and conserved your energy, you will be ready to push on to the finish. At the final feed station fill your bottles, take a gel and eat, as you will be getting back on the bike with the aim of finishing as fast as possible.

You will be feeling tired; you may have aches that you never dreamed possible, but we can assure you that you can push your body harder than you ever imagined. Colin Chapman, the famous car designer and founder of Lotus cars, once famously said that 'car drivers drive at only 30 per cent of the capability of the car'. Bike riders are the same; the ability to push beyond your perceived limits is a psychological, not a physical limit in almost all cases.

The last third of an event can also be a time to be extra vigilant in terms of your concentration, bike handling and position with other riders. Different people react to tiredness in different ways, but physical and mental exhaustion can sometimes mean that riders will do unexpected things. The key here is to expect the unexpected and ride defensively where required. Examples are talking to your fellow riders to signify you intend to make a manoeuvre, talking to them to make sure you work as a cohesive group, or merely shouting encouragement to a member of the group who may be tiring. A common mistake is for riders to be head down and miss a turn – this is of course especially dangerous on left-hand turns if they fail to turn and you cut across in front of them. Watch out especially at the final feed station, as some riders will be riding through and not stopping.

You may also find that groups become smaller as you near the end of the ride. Different terrain will have split the larger groups into smaller clusters of two, three or four riders. This can be a really satisfying time in a ride, as collectively you are all on the limit, but you can really help each other by sharing the workload and dragging each other to a better time. We have met some really great riding companions from the common bond of exhaustion and the lure of the finishing line.

Your aim should be to cross the finish line with nothing left to give but without collapsing and needing oxygen – if you get it right, there is no better sense of satisfaction, and many of you will experience high emotions at the sense of achievement.

Unexpected Events

If you have prepared well, are carrying the right food and have checked your equipment, the chances are that you will have a trouble-free ride. If, however, you do encounter a problem, it is important to remain calm. This is easier said than done in the middle of an event, where you will feel every minute lost will be a waste of your hard work or a threat to your pre-event goals.

With accidents in mind it is always a good idea to carry some sort of ID on you during an event. Most sportives will ask you to write the details of next of kin on the back of your number bib, but we recommend you take this into your hands and wear an ID tag or bracelet. We personally wear a bracelet from Road I.D. (www.roadid.com) that carries next of kin, phone number, date of birth, blood group and allergy information. We also wear this whenever we ride, especially alone, because if anything were to happen it provides a very quick way to identify you to anyone providing help in an emergency.

Coping With Accidents

Accidents do happen, and you would be a very lucky cyclist if you trained and competed regularly and never fell off the bike. Some statistician once worked out that the average high-mileage cyclist falls off every 7,200km at least, so in our case, that's two tumbles a year. We feel we should say a few words about falling off and crashing in the hope that we can minimize the effects when it happens.

First, try to avoid crashes in the first place. Stay very vigilant and aware, especially when riding in a group. Constantly scan the area ahead and around you, and develop an awareness of what other riders are doing, and how they ride. Pay close attention to the road surface ahead of you, especially these days when there are serious pot-holes on most roads, in the UK particularly. With many hundreds or thousands of miles under your belt you will develop a 'sixth sense' about certain situations which will serve you well – but eventually something will happen and you will fall.

Going Down

As the crash happens, try to minimize damage by falling as safely as possible – although probably you will have little time to react and think, and there may be others around you whose actions are beyond your control. Try to curl as you fall, and if at all possible, fall and slide rather than take a downward crunch; if you can at least just slide along the road you are more likely to suffer merely abrasions rather than breakages. In extreme situations it is sometimes even sensible to 'lay the bike down', as a motorcyclist would put it, rather than hit something head on.

Strange as it may seem, crashing at speed is often preferable to a slow speed accident, as you can use your forward momentum to dissipate the impact. Most relatively minor cycling injuries are to the hands, arms and shoulder areas, and many are caused by very low speed crashes as the falling rider stretches an arm out to break the fall, or hits the ground with the point of the shoulder. Most of the time, cycling accidents result in relatively superficial injuries, which shouldn't stop you continuing the ride; however, occasionally the consequences are more serious.

Recognize when you should pull out, and never risk further complications or damage by trying to ride through a severe injury.

Reaction and Treatment

Once you have come to a halt after the tumble, and assuming you are still conscious, alert and mobile (albeit smarting a bit), pick yourself up and quickly get yourself out of the way of any other cyclists or road users.

Next begin to check the damage, first to yourself, then to your machine. Gently move your limbs and check that you have a full range of movement, even if this is uncomfortable and painful. If you detect something more serious, causing restricted movement and acute pain, stop moving and think about calling for help. If, however, you can move everything and feel fully aware of your surroundings, then take a look at the bike, in particular at wheels and handlebars. Check that everything functions and is safe.

If you feel that the bike is still roadworthy and you are able to continue, then the best thing to do is probably to get on and start to pedal, slowly and carefully, still checking that nothing is acutely damaged around your body. In many cases after a crash you will experience a massive adrenalin rush, which will propel you forwards through the pain barrier. If you can ride without causing further injury, then do ride, as the circulation of blood and nutrients will actually be beneficial to the healing process.

But let us sound a note of caution here – do not continue if you are experiencing specific, acute pain, or if you have pronounced loss of mobility. And don't ride a bike that is unsafe.

Once you get back to base or home, make sure you treat the inevitable consequences properly. If you have 'road rash' and abrasions, then make sure, painful though it is, that you clean the wounds thoroughly and apply some antiseptic cream or ointment. Then just take it steady for a while, practising the classic technique of 'RICE' as appropriate:

- **Rest:** Take it easy and let your body start to heal itself
- **Ice:** Apply ice to swollen areas to reduce inflammation and swelling
- **Compression:** Useful for increasing blood flow to injured areas, and speeding up healing
- **Elevation:** To prevent 'pooling' of fluids in injured areas.

Take a few days off the bike after a nasty fall, and let your body recover and repair itself; only if you have very minor scrapes and bruises should you ride gently to keep the blood and nutrients flowing, and if you have access to a static bike, maybe that should be your preferred riding machine for a couple of days.

There will be some mental damage as well: only a few people can crash and then forget it instantly, erasing it from memory. But however vivid the memory of the accident, just like horse-riding it is important to get up, get back on the bike and ride again. Put the accident in context, and move on.

Punctures

The most common technical problem while riding a sportive is a puncture. When this happens it is important to come to a stop as soon as is practicable to get out of the way of other riders and vehicles. If you are riding in a group shout 'puncture' and (if possible) raise an arm as you slow down to give your riding partners time either to stop themselves or to ride round you safely.

Once you have stopped you should repair the puncture in a methodical, slow manner. Rushing generally means you will miss, forget or not check something, and this usually results in a second puncture shortly after setting off because you failed to remove the nail/stone/thorn that caused the initial puncture, or you 'pinched' the tube between the tyre and the rim. Remember to fold up your used inner tube and place it into your saddle bag or jersey pocket – do not leave it at the roadside.

Some cyclists recommend a CO_2 canister pump for the first repair as this enables you to pump up your tyre instantly (practise with one first), but check whether you can take it on your flight if you are going abroad.

Speed Wobble

On certain descents it is possible to experience a most disconcerting problem often referred to as 'speed wobble'. Your bike will vibrate, making you feel as if the front wheel is falling off, and the handlebars will start to shake in your hands. The first time this happens it is not pleasant, to say the least. The instinctive reaction is to brake hard, but often this can exacerbate the problem. The wobble can be controlled by doing three things:

- Position the pedals parallel to the ground and 'grip' the top tube with your knees to give stability. This will change the dynamics of the frame and calm the vibration
- Lightly apply both front and rear brake at the same time to reduce your speed
- Avoid any sudden movements that may add to the problem.

As your speed reduces the speed wobble should disappear, and you will be riding normally. This is an extremely rare occurrence, but it is worth knowing what to do should you experience it. Once you get home, check the bike for any faults such as a broken spoke or a slight wheel buckle, and check that the brakes are applying evenly.

FIXING A PUNCTURE

With the right preparation and only a little patience, a puncture is easy to fix and can be done in a very few minutes:

- First rule: carry a spare inner tube and the tools to do the job. On the road it's far easier to change the tube and repair the punctured one later. Carry some self-stick patches in case of a second puncture. You will need a set of tyre levers and a pump as well
- Stand the bike upside down. Open up the brake calipers and take off the wheel using the quick-release lever on the hub

Place the bike upside down and remove the wheel.

- Slip the flat end of a tyre lever between the rim and the tyre, bend it back and hook it on to one of the spokes to hold it in place if necessary. Take the next lever and do the same about 8cm further around the tyre. Either slide the second lever around the rim to release the tyre off the rim, or remove the first lever then move it further along the rim and use it to pry off the tyre again until one side is completely free
- Take the punctured inner tube out. Take the tyre fully off the rim around one side and inspect the inside by sight as well as by running your fingers inside and outside to establish the cause of the flat, or for any other unwanted glass, flints or thorns that may have caused the puncture

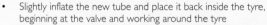

Removing the tyre takes care and attention.

- Slightly inflate the new tube and place it back inside the tyre, beginning at the valve and working around the tyre
- Begin putting the tyre back inside the rim using your thumb to place the tyre edge over the rim edge. Start near the valve and work round in opposite directions. For the last part you may need to use your tyre levers, too; be careful not to pinch the inner tube as you finish the procedure
- Pump up the tyre to as close to your starting pressure as possible. Replace your tyre levers into your saddle bag, fold the old tube into your bag or place in your rear jersey pocket – don't just throw it away.

It is absolutely worth practising puncture repairs at home over the dark days of winter as it is quite possible to reduce the time it takes to less than five minutes. It is a basic skill required of any rider.

ABOVE: Use your thumbs to lever the tyre back on.

LEFT: Check the inside of the tyre for any damage or foreign body that might be the source of the puncture.

'The Bonk'

If you do not eat or drink correctly you may experience the dreaded 'bonk': light-headedness, loss of power, extreme tiredness and an inability to maintain anything near your previous speed. It can happen to anyone – even to Lance Armstrong, seven-time winner of the Tour de France during the 2009 Paris–Nice race. He had forgotten to eat at a crucial part of a stage and was subsequently dropped, losing minutes, and struggling to finish.

If you begin to experience symptoms of the bonk, then check what food and drink you have on you. Consume what you have, especially bananas, gel or energy bars, which are fast-release energy sources. If you are riding with a friend, ask if they have any spare food or drinks. It is important to get to the next food station (or the end of the event if you suffer the feeling towards the end) as soon as possible so that you can take on fuel.

The bonk will affect your sense of awareness and balance, so be extremely careful of riding on if you feel very weak. If this is the case, then pull over and find a place to rest (in the shade). If you are riding in mainland Europe then you might even stop at a café and eat a sandwich with a coffee or coke, and refill your bottles with water. The time spent doing this will pay dividends in terms of your own personal safety and ability to finish the event.

The good news is that you will recover from this condition very quickly once you have ingested food: a banana, energy bar or gel will bring about an improvement in your condition within minutes.

Experience Says …

- Accept your starting position. Don't fret about where you are at the start
- Eat a good breakfast two to three hours before the start in order to let your body digest the fuel
- In cold conditions early on, wear a pair of thin rubber surgical gloves beneath your cycling gloves; remove them at the first feed station as the temperature rises
- Your legs may feel dead for the first 20km – don't worry, ride through it and your feeling of strength will come back
- Do not miss feed stations, but don't hang around in them, either
- Split the event into thirds: ride smoothly over the first third, consolidate in the second, and give it all you have over the final third
- Start eating early, and eat little and often during the event
- Eat on flat and downhill sections – it's easier than trying to eat whilst struggling up a climb
- Stay hydrated – drink every 10 minutes; 5 per cent dehydration results in 20 per cent power loss
- Don't chase too hard at the start – ride at your own pace and look for riders or groups of similar abilities
- Deal with accidents and incidents as they arise; don't fret about things you can't control.

CHAPTER 10

POST-EVENT RECOVERY

It is to be hoped that the hours and miles of training and preparation have paid off, and you have achieved your goal. The next event is in the schedule, and you want to do even better in that one. But before you head out and start putting in more miles at even higher intensity, think about giving your 'engine' some time off to recuperate and recover. To achieve good performances all through the season your body needs to take time to rest, recover, repair and adapt after the exertions of an endurance event such as a sportive.

Establishing a recovery programme is as important as putting together a training plan, and getting the balance right between recovery rides and training between events is essential if you are to progress. The first stage of recovery is rest, and although each individual is different, in general terms the following chart shows how much recovery time is required after a specific event or training session. The recovery times suggested are a minimum, and some riders will need longer recovery periods.

REQUIRED RECOVERY TIMES

Activity	Recovery needed
Continuous aerobic effort 6hr duration	8hr
One hour tempo training	8hr
2hr high tempo session	24 to 30hr
Lactate session, 30min duration	24hr
Lactate/endurance session of 90min	24hr
30min high intensity above lactate threshold	24hr

Active Recovery

You may be surprised at just how long a relatively short training session needs in terms of recovery, and we're certainly not suggesting that after each session you stay off the bike completely; but after a hard effort it is necessary to put in either a rest day or a recovery ride at very light intensity and low heart rate. If you choose the latter, then what you are trying to achieve is 'active recovery', which is designed only to exert enough effort to stimulate recovery and spin out lactate in the muscles, but not enough to put undue load on the body.

A typical recovery ride might, for example, last an hour or so at a heart rate of 60 per cent of maximum, pedalling at an average cadence of 75rpm. You will stimulate blood flow to deliver the nutrients required for recovery, and generally let the body work gently in the background to repair any damage and begin to adapt after training or competition. Note that if you are in the middle of some power or other high intensity sessions such as lactate threshold intervals you will need a greater recovery period than when putting in lower intensity base miles.

Bear in mind that the body also needs to replenish its fuel stores, starting immediately after the event with a meal or carbohydrate/protein recovery drink within the first thirty minutes. This refuelling period is called the glycogen window, in which the enzymes which produce glycogen are at their most active and the ingestion of protein stimulates the effect of insulin on transporting blood sugars back to the muscles.

Don't forget to drink and replace electrolytes lost by sweating and the physiological processes involved in hard effort over a long period. You will have depleted minerals including sodium, magnesium, calcium and potassium, and these need to be replaced. Their purpose in the body is to initiate and activate muscle contraction and relaxation, and it is the loss of these elements that lead to muscle cramps and fatigue.

Finally, and we have discussed the importance of this in an earlier section, you need to sleep and allow your body – and your mind – the opportunity to regenerate and repair itself for as long as it takes; for most of us that means at least eight hours a night while engaging in a programme of training or competition.

Recovery Overview

It is important to remember that training and competing is a cyclical and repetitious process, involving periods of activity, sometimes intense, followed by periods of rest and regeneration. After a major event it is absolutely right to take some time out to reflect and consider the whole experience. If that experience has left you drained, then rest for a while longer, gently spinning to maintain base fitness. If it has left you, as it usually does, keen and ready to aim for the next challenge, then identify the event, build the programme and re-read the book to acquire even more knowledge before the next effort. Ask questions of more experienced riders, try to analyse and understand how you rode, what your limitations and issues were, and try to improve areas of weakness through even more specific and accurate training and preparation.

CHAPTER 11

FREQUENTLY ASKED QUESTIONS

Over the years we have brought a number of friends, acquaintances and business contacts into the world of cycling and sportive riding in particular. Some of them were novices to both cycling and sportive riding, and we have tried to help them gain knowledge and experience as they built their fitness and their ambitions. One or two of them now regularly ride with us over the most challenging and demanding courses, and as we train throughout the 'off' season. In writing this book we have tried to cover the topics we felt were most relevant to the new sportive rider or to the cyclist looking to improve times and performances; we hope we have covered most areas and given you a better understanding of some of the techniques and approaches we have been taught by others or have found out the hard way, by trial and error.

Before we close the final chapter and let you begin the next stage of your sportive career, we thought it would be useful to encapsulate, in short, sharp question and answer format, the snippets of information that seem to occur time and time again.

So here are some of the questions that newcomers to cycling and sportives frequently ask us, and our answers to them:

Q. I am new to cycling – will I be able to tackle a sportive?
A. Yes, with this book, the right bike, the right equipment, a training plan and the right mental attitude most physically active people could complete an average sportive.

Q. Where do I find out what events are happening, and where they are?
A. We suggest using www.cyclosport.org or the *Cycling Weekly* website, www.cyclingweekly.com.

Q. What kind of bike do I need?
A. For a newcomer we recommend buying a pre-specified sportive road bike from a major manufacturer, costing (at the time of writing) between £600 and £1,000. It will probably have compact gearing, meaning front rings of 50/34 and rear cogs of 12/28 or 13/29.

Q. What other equipment will I need?
A. We recommend that you carry a seat pack with spare tube, tyre levers and allen keys, as well as a pump on the bike frame. We also recommend that you fit clipless pedals, as these allow you to pedal more effectively. You will improve your training if you use a cycle computer/heart rate monitor to measure and record progress.

Q. What clothes should I wear for the event?
A. This depends on the weather conditions, but remember that things can change in the space of a few hours. So even if you are able to wear a short-sleeve jersey and shorts, carry a wind- and rainproof top, and consider using arm and knee warmers at the start.

Q. What food do I need for the ride?
A. You could carry some basic items including energy bars, bananas, dried fruit and energy gels, and fill your water bottles with diluted energy drink.

Q. What kind of training should I do?
A. This will depend on your level of base fitness, but basically at the beginning of your programme you should concentrate on steady paced, distance work, then progress to include some intervals of higher intensity riding.

Q. How many miles do I need to ride?
A. This will depend on the event you have chosen, but for, say, an 130km sportive you will need to be building up over a few months to a minimum of 120km or more a week to train properly. The mileage should include one or two longer rides as well to accustom you to long periods in the saddle.

Q. What are the most important aspects of training and preparation?
A. Choosing an appropriate bike that fits properly, doing the right amount of mileage, riding some reasonably long distances, maintaining a healthy diet with the right proportions of carbohydrate, protein and fat, and making sure you get enough recovery time between rides.

Q. What time should I aim for?
A. Again, this depends on the sportive, but over an average course with some climbing involved, if you can maintain an average speed of 22km/h or more, you'll be doing fine. The more experienced, fitter riders will aim for 27km/h or faster. The important thing is to start out at a sensible pace and ride your own race.

Q. What mistakes will negatively affect my performance the most?

A. Trying to ride too quickly, too early, not eating and drinking enough, hanging around in feed stations, and not working with other riders to share the workload.

Q. What's the most important aspect of preparation for an event?

A. Make travel and accommodation arrangements early, make checklists of things you will take with you, register as early as possible, get plenty of rest the night before, and don't worry about your start position when you get there.

Q. What are the most important things I can do to ride faster?

A. Assuming you have the right training programme, which builds on all aspects of riding and technique, then losing some weight and building some leg power will make the biggest difference to your time.

Q. I haven't really ridden in a group before; what are the most important things to remember when I join other riders during an event?

A. Stay vigilant, don't brake suddenly, and use clear signs and calls to let people know what's happening.

Q. I am a nervous descender and haven't ridden fast down long descents before. What should I remember?

A. Try to anticipate what's up ahead, and look out in front of you to find your exit on bends. Don't brake too suddenly, and shift your weight backwards to keep the bike stable.

CHAPTER 12

THE FINAL WORD

This book will have given you the opportunity to develop the skills you already possess and perhaps to correct or amend some thoughts, ideas and habits that may have been formed over time. We have enjoyed putting it together, and have learned much ourselves in the process through the research and reading we have done. When all is said and done, choosing to ride a sportive is more than an outing on a bicycle; we are all on a personal journey to challenge ourselves and push beyond our normal comfort zone, seeking an achievement that translates positively across the rest of what we do and how we live in our day-to-day lives.

Sportives give us the opportunity to join like-minded riders of all ages and abilities in the pursuit of personal achievement and success over challenging courses in some spectacular locations. The biggest and best of them also give us a taste of what the pro riders experience as they train, prepare and race at incredible speeds around the globe.

To complete a tough sportive successfully demands that the rider achieves a level of fitness, bike skills and ability, and displays mental and physical toughness exploring areas of personal capability which may not have been tested before. The personal satisfaction gained from completing an event or beating a target time often translates into other parts of our lives, building confidence and motivation. Camaraderie on the road and the support of spectators and organizers add to the overall experience and enhance the personal reward from the event.

But a note of caution: like road racing and time trialling, the future of our freedom on the road depends on the support and tolerance of many sections of the wider community, including organizers, other road users and the general public. We all need to be aware of the impact of our riding and behaviour in a wider context. For example, nowadays almost every sportive route is littered with gel sachets, energy bar wrappers and discarded inner tubes and litter. Surely, if it was acceptable to carry all this at the start of the event, it's possible for us to carry it back to the finish?

We need to respect the environment and the right of local people to enjoy their roads without our rubbish – and remember, when it comes to a conflict, a car is bigger, heavier and faster than a sportive rider and a bike, so there is only one loser in a contest of aggression between the two.

We hope you have enjoyed reading this book, and that some of our experience is of value to you as you prepare for your next event. We have enjoyed many years and many hours and miles of challenging and scenic riding, and we look forward to welcoming you to the world of sportive.

From both of us: ride safely, ride strongly and enjoy your sportive career.

GLOSSARY

Like any sport or activity, cycling has its own language and its own special terms. To the newcomer, these can seem like an impenetrable barrier that prevents you feeling as if you belong to 'the club'. This section should dispel some of the mystery, and help you become familiar with the words and terms that you hear all the time in the sport. Some of the terms we list aren't necessarily used in the book; we just felt it would be useful to have a reference point to let you understand the language of cyclists.

abdominal Relating to the muscles and body area around your middle.

adaptation The process of building more physical capability in response to training.

aero bars Handlebars, or clip-on bars, which allow a more aerodynamic position.

aerobic The state before oxygen debt occurs and lactate acid accumulates.

aerobic capacity The range at which a cyclist can work before going anaerobic.

aerodynamic A streamlined position to reduce wind resistance.

anaerobic Beyond aerobic: lactic acid accumulates, and oxygen debt occurs.

allen key Hexagonal tool for tightening bolts.

ankling Rotating or turning the ankle at the end of the push.

antioxidant A substance that counteracts the negative effects of free radicals.

apex The point in a corner or bend at its most curved.

arm warmers Removable extensions to a jersey to preserve warmth.

bar hooks The lower, curved part of the handlebar.

base (fitness) The endurance platform built by training.

bidon Water bottle.

bib ¾ Tights that end just below the knee.

bib shorts Shorts with shoulder straps and protection for the kidneys and middle.

bib tights/bib longs Full-length version of the above.

biomechanics The way the body moves and functions mechanically.

body mass index (BMI) An indicator related to power/weight and body fat.

body mineral density (BMD) An indicator of bone health and density.

bonk Point at which the body runs out of fuel during exertion.

bottom bracket The circular part of the lower frame where the axle is located.

brake block The rubber part of the braking system.

brake lever The part that is gripped by the hand to initiate braking.

brake shoes The housing for the brake blocks.

broom wagon The vehicle that sweeps up slow or retired riders.

bunny hop A useful manoeuvre to jump over small obstacles/potholes.

cadence The number of pedal revolutions (in a minute).

cage Water-bottle holder fixed to the down tube.

captain The front person on a tandem.

carbohydrate   The essential fuel for the endurance cyclist – simple and complex sugars.

carbo-loading   Eating greater quantities of carbohydrate before an event.

cardiovascular   The system that transports blood around the body.

cassette   The collection of small gears/sprockets at the rear of the bike.

chainring   The front drive rings connected to the pedals.

chain set   The collective name for rings, cassette, chain.

chain stay   Frame section below the chain from the bottom bracket to the rear wheel.

cleat   Attached to the shoe and clips into the pedals.

clincher   A wheel that uses a tyre with an inner tube.

clipless   A pedal system that clips shoe and pedal together.

CO₂ (cartridge)   Used to inflate a repaired tyre.

core (strength)   Abdominal strength around the midriff.

crank (arm)   The lever that connects the chainring to the pedal.

criterium   A local race often held in the evening.

C to C   A standard frame measurement: centre of frame to centre of frame.

cyclosportive   A mass-participation cycling event.

deep section   Aerodynamic wheels with wide rims.

derailleur   The mechanisms attached to the frame which shift gears and chainrings.

down tube   The frame tube from the head tube to the bottom bracket.

drafting   Sitting behind another rider to reduce wind resistance.

drops   The lower part of the handlebars.

dust cap   Cover that screws on to the tyre valve.

echelon   A formation of riders in a crosswind.

electrolytes   Minerals essential for muscle contraction and relaxation.

energy bar   Concentrated high-calorie nutrition for events.

feathering   Lightly applying and releasing brakes.

feed station   Location of food and water during an event.

fixed gear   One gear, connected direct to the chainring; no freewheeling possible.

flywheel   Small 'jockey' wheel in rear derailleur.

forks   Frame section holding front wheel in place.

frame set   Collective term for frame with headset and forks.

free radicals   Damaging chemicals produced as a by-product of exercise.

front mech/derailleur   Mechanism that shifts chain.

gel   High calorie, easily ingested fuel for events.

gilet   Form of waistcoat for wind protection.

gluteal (muscles)   Muscles of the posterior/bottom.

glycaemic (index)   A measure of the effects of carbohydrates on blood sugar levels.

glycogen   Carbohydrate/sugar stored and used by the muscles in exercise.

granny gears   The smallest sprockets in the cassette.

grimpeur   A rider particularly suited to climbing hills/mountains.

group set   Collective term for gears, brakes, chainrings, cassette, cables.

hamstrings   Muscles at the back of the upper leg.

handlebars   Points by which to grip the bike and control direction.

headset   Screw or integrated section that connects the handlebars to the forks.

head tube   Section of frame at the front below the bars.

hip flexor   Upper leg muscles controlling rising/falling movement.

hot foot   Pain caused by pressure points in shoes.

HRM   Heart rate monitor for measuring heart rate.

hub   The component around which the wheel spins.

hydration   Maintaining water/fluids in the body.

inner tube   The thin rubber inner section of the tyre holding the air.

insulin   Hormone that helps transport glucose from blood to muscles.

intensity   The level of effort at which training is taking place.

intervals   Training sessions where varying effort and intensity are applied.

knee warmers   Removable protection for the knees.

lactate   Lactic acid, which impedes and inhibits muscle contraction.

lactate threshold   The level at which your body cannot remove lactic acid.

lug   The area where the frame tubes connect and join.

mash   To push a big chainring or gear rather than 'spinning' at higher cadence.

maximum hr   The maximum beats of the heart.

mid-section   Semi-aerodynamic wheel rims.

mini tool   Device with various bike tools in one unit.

mitts   Short- or long-fingered cycling gloves.

musette   A small bag, worn over the shoulder when riding, containing food to eat while riding.

over-extension   When the seat is too high causing the leg to be too straight.

overload (training)   Applying greater training strain to cause muscles to grow.

overshoes   Covers placed over your cycling shoes to protect the feet from cold and wet.

patch   Small piece of rubber for puncture repair.

peloton   Describes groups of riders in an event.

perineum   The sensitive area under the crotch.

periodization   Training in specific patterns of effort and time.

power-to-weight (ratio)   Muscle power output related to bodyweight.

profile   The shape of the rider on the bike.

protein   Fuel source essential for tissue repair and growth.

psi (pounds per square inch)   A measure of tyre pressure.

quadriceps   Group of large muscles in the upper leg area above the knee.

randonnee cyclosportive   The original term for a long-distance sportive-style event.

reach   The distance from saddle to handlebars.

rear mech/derailleur   The device that moves the chain up and down the cassette.

recumbent   A bicycle with the rider lying backwards and the legs facing forwards.

repeats   Training technique of repeated efforts on a hill, for example.

resting hr   Number of heart beats when not exercising or moving around.

RICE   Term used in recovery from injury. Stands for rest, ice, compression and elevation.

rim   The outside of the wheel that houses the tyre.

road rash   Abrasion injuries as skin is torn away on impact with road surface.

rollers   Training aid on which the bike is balanced and pedalled without being secured.

saddle   Resting place for your bottom.

saddle setback   Distance the saddle is positioned on the saddle rails.

saddle tilt   Angle of the saddle on the saddle rails.

saturated fat   A fat, most often of animal origin, that is solid at room temperature. Excess amounts in your diet raises cholesterol in the bloodstream.

seat clamp   The mechanism to tighten the seat post.

seat post   The post that connects the saddle to the frame.

seat stays   The long frame tubes connecting the saddle area to the rear wheel.

seat tube   The long vertical tube from the saddle area to the bottom bracket.

shifter   Handlebar-mounted device for changing gear.

skewer   Run through the wheel hubs and secure wheels in the frame dropouts.

spacer   On the headset, used to raise or lower handle-bars.

spin   Pedal lightly at a high cadence.

speed wobble   At speed on a descent, the bike feels as if it is moving from side to side out of your control.

spokes   Thin metal rods connecting the wheel hub to the wheel rim.

sportive   Mass-participation cycling event.

sprockets   Small gears making up the rear cassette.

steerer tube   Long tube that connects the headset/bars to the forks.

stem   Centrepiece of the handlebars connected to the headset.

STI (shifter)   Handlebar-mounted device for changing gears.

stoker   Rear rider on a tandem.

supplement   Substance taken to augment food.

tandem   Bicycle made for two.

taper   Progressively reduce training before an event.

tempo   High cadence or high intensity training technique.

threadless   Modern method of connecting handlebars/steerer tube to the forks.

through and off   When group riding, as a rider reaches the front, he peels off, allowing another rider to lead.

the tops   Top of the brake hoods.

time trial   Solo timed event against the clock.

tpi (tread per inch)   A measure of tyre tread patterns.

top tube   The horizontal tube from the saddle area to the handlebar area.

torque wrench   A device for tightening bolts to precise levels.

training zone   Heart-rate zone between two specific levels.

tubular   A wheel/tyre that does not need an inner tube.

turbo trainer   A stationary device that, using a resistance hub, allows you to ride your bike indoors for training purposes.

tyre lever   For removing a tyre from the rim.

tyre valve   For connecting the pump to inflate the tyre.

visualization   Technique for imagining success.

VO$_2$ Measure of the amount of oxygen a person can breathe in and use for aerobic power.

wicking   Transferring sweat away from the body.

wind resistance   The force or pressure of the wind against the rider.

wheel sucker   A rider who does not do their turn on the front, but sits on your wheel benefiting from the draught you are creating.

APPENDIX I

British Cycling Rules, Cyclosportives

British Cycling rules as at 1 December 2006: regulations for BC cycling for all (cyclo-sportive/tourist) events:

These Events will be known as 'Cycling for All' events. All paperwork produced will state 'Under British Cycling Cyclo-sportive/Tourist Regulations'.

Every Event will carry the BCF Event Insurance (on payment of the appropriate fee by the organiser) which will cover the club, the promoter, other officers of the club, the event officials and all participants for the duration of the event against any claims from a third party.

Participants will be responsible for the roadworthiness of their own cycle.

Groups of participants on the road may not be of more than twenty riders. These groups must start a minimum of two minutes apart. All participants will at all times obey the laws of the road. Failure to do so will result in automatic disqualification from the event.

The organizer will ensure that the course is checked within forty-eight hours prior to the event, and any danger points advised to each participant on the day. A risk assessment of the event must be completed for the proposed route.

The organizer shall wherever possible select a route that is low in traffic volumes and away from major towns. These routes should be attractive to the participant and be designed to suit their level of competence. When choosing a suitable route, consideration should be given to finding a hill early in the event to alleviate the possibility of bunches forming that are greater than twenty riders. The use of larger main roads close to the start can achieve the same objective.

Where possible, route markers will be used to identify the route to be taken. However, it is the responsibility of each participant to take the correct course.

Controls on the route will be set up at the farthest points of the course to reduce claims of riders not covering the correct route. At each control the participant will have the control card/transponder marked to show the time of arrival.

No accompanying vehicles are allowed to follow riders.

There will be no list published which indicates a finishing position or time other than which standard was achieved by which riders. An alphabetical list of finishers and times is a preferred format.

The wearing of hard shell style helmets shall be compulsory for junior and youth riders. Senior riders are encouraged to do the same.

All participants under the age of eighteen shall have had a consent form completed by their parent/guardian.

It is advised that all riders must carry a form of identification showing their name, address and contact details of the person to be advised in the eventuality of an accident. It is also advised that all participants carry enough food, drink, money and extra clothing to complete the ride being undertaken, taking into account the route and possible adverse weather conditions.

The organizer has the option to take entries on the line as well as in advance. An increase in the entry fee may be charged for this privilege at the discretion of the organizer.

The organizer is encouraged to supply mechanical or refreshment support services to participants.

Organizers are encouraged to advise the local police station(s) in writing of the existence of the event, giving details of the route, approximate timings and numbers involved. A copy of these regulations should also be enclosed.

APPENDIX II

Travel and Equipment List for Air Travel

Bike and Equipment

- Bike dismantled
- Pedals and other removable items packed in shoes
- Handlebars loosened and taken off head tube if necessary, tucked under frame
- Frame tubes protected by pipe lagging
- Chain/derailleur wrapped in cloth and taped
- Saddle/seat post out and tied to frame (re-tighten seat-post clamp)
- Carbohydrate powder and gels in freezer bags and inside water bottles (back in cages)
- Helmet, sunglasses, gloves, other soft items in helmet bag
- Shoes with spares, tools, gels, and fastened to secure
- Track or other pump if space/weight allows
- Tyres deflated.

Clothing and Gear

- Short-sleeve jersey – long zip if hot season/climbing in heat
- Long-sleeve jersey and/or arm warmers
- Windproof gilet
- Bib shorts and knee warmers and/or
- Three-quarter bibs and/or
- Long-bib tights
- Thermal-base layer
- Water-/windproof jacket
- Socks × 2
- Cycling mitts and/or
- Long-finger gloves
- Overshoes.

Accessories and Spares

- Chamois cream
- Sun protection
- Bike computer/watch/GPS
- Inner tubes × 2
- Tyre levers × 2
- Allen keys/spanners
- Self-glue puncture patches × 2
- Warming oil
- Prescription medicines, anti-inflammatories, pain relief tablets
- Contact lenses and cleaning items.

INDEX

RELATED TITLES FROM CROWOOD

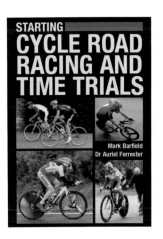

Starting Cycle Road Racing and Time Trials

MARK BARFIELD & AURIEL FORRESTER

ISBN 978 1 84797 014 5

112pp, 80 illustrations

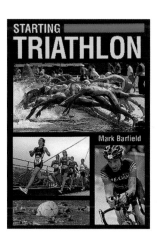

Starting Triathlon

MARK BARFIELD

ISBN 978 1 86126 875 4

144pp, 100 illustrations

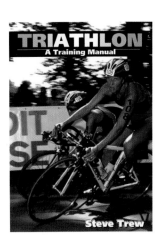

Triathlon A Training Manual

STEVE TREW

ISBN 978 1 86126 386 5

224pp, 70 illustrations

Triathlon Crowood Sports Guide

STEVE TREW

ISBN 978 1 84797 170 8

96pp, 100 illustrations

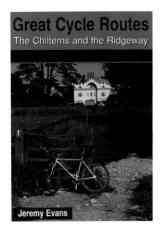

Great Cycle Routes The Chilterns and the Ridgeway

JEREMY EVANS

ISBN 978 1 86126 029 1

96pp, 50 illustrations

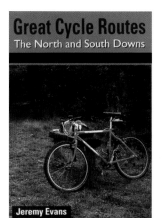

Great Cycle Routes The North and South Downs

JEREMY EVANS

ISBN 978 1 85223 850 6

96pp, 50 illustrations